Scrumptious Self Care

Marilyn Idle

Scrumptious Self Care
New Title, Same Classic Book © June 2014

Original Title: Scrumptious Care ... *After You Read This Book, You Will Feel Better Than Before You Read It* ©2010
Edition: First, American Version, August 2010
        Second, Updated September 2011
Authored by: Marilyn Idle
Copyright by: Marilyn Idle
Editor: Catherine Hart Communications, Writing, Editing, Publicity, PO Box 1454, Taos, NM 87571, groove@mcn.org
Photographer: Laureen McLean
Photographer: Karlee Bowman
Photo Licenses: Istockphoto.com

Publisher: Marilyn Idle, www.marilynidle.com
Retail Order information, Publishing Inquiry or Permissions for Reprints: Marilyn Idle, P.O. Box 484, Christina Lake, BC, Canada V0H 1E0

Classification: Non-fiction
Key Search words: Marilyn Idle, Scrumptious Self Care, Self-care, Coupleship, Relationship, Self-massage, Self-healing, Body/Mind/Spirit, Health and Healing, Self-help, Laughter

Related Tips and Articles: http://www.MarilynIdle.com http:www.ScrumptiousCare.com
To purchase online: Search for by title **Scrumptious Self Care** or search by author name Marilyn Idle

Disclaimer: Readers are responsible for their use of the tips in this book and their life decisions.
Note: Nothing on this page impairs or restricts the author's moral rights.
Claim: All that may be perceived as "imperfections" within this book were done on purpose.

ISBN-13: 978-1500355913
ISBN-10: 1500355917
BISAC: Self-Help / Self-Management / Stress Management

Dedication

This book is dedicated to Laurel Thom. She taught me her knowledge of the precious art of care, which for me is the way to be human and infinite pure love—at the same time.

About Marilyn Idle

Marilyn Idle is a wellness advocate for people and Earth's biosphere. With a degree in law and background in advocacy, mediation and counselling, she shares her insights for self and planetary healing through connection with life force or *chi* and nature. Lovingly and caringly, she teaches daily simple and soothing self-care techniques that generate tranquility, comfort, and balance for you and those you care about.

Acknowledgements

To all families, mothers, fathers, grandmothers, grandfathers, brothers and sisters: This book is for everyone, especially all of the children.

In gratitude to life, to Paul, to Nathan. Thank you for your love and being there with smiles, hugs, and humor.

To my mom Elizabeth and her life partner George, my dad Bud and his wife Anne and my stepdad John and his wife Justine: I love you.

To my whole family and many universal friends I've met along the way. Thank you for sharing a stage of finite-life on Earth within the unconditional love of infinity.

To those who read this book, thank you for reading it ... this book was written for *you* and for those you care about and love.

—Marilyn Idle

Preface

This book is a living, breathing document. It is not a beginning-to-end kind of book, which one would read only cover-to-cover. This is a book to keep near and dear, on your bedside table, coffee table, by your computer, or in your purse or briefcase, opening it anytime, to any page. You will find self-care ideas for your body, family, relationships, and the Earth.

Within eighteen elegant chapters, Marilyn shares hundreds of useful down-to-earth tips for self, family and couple care, a myriad of uplifting and humorous quotes and stories, beautiful photos, plus over twenty delectable organic food recipes.

As questions come up for you, self-care is all about seeking further input until you find *your own* answers, and at the same time remembering—you are never alone. In these pages you will find ideas to uplift, amuse, and make you ponder—you may even come down with a case of *contagious wellness*!

Proviso

The ideas in this book are from the opinions, research, and life experiences of the author. Marilyn is not an expert and certainly would never claim to be one in regards to you, your body, or your life. Because we are each different, it is important that you choose what is best for you and change or delete what is not. You are the one you have been waiting for. As with any important life decisions involving your wellness, if you are uncertain, check with a trusted person or health professional before implementing exercises or ideas. Otherwise, enjoy!

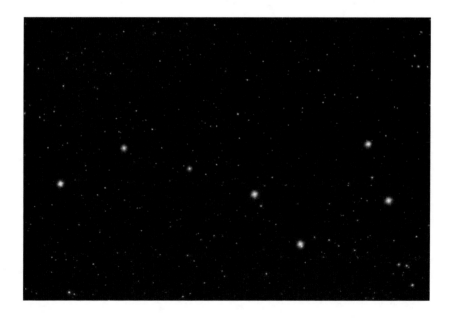

Contents

Introduction

If the human race *ever* had natural and simple self-care techniques to use daily to remain strong and well, it seems lately that many people have gone without them—I certainly had. With modern advances in technology, life ought to be simpler and people more relaxed; yet we are more stressed and work harder and longer. "Do more" fixes are offered, such as time-consuming and unrealistic hours-per-day indoor workouts and expensive medications and treatments, yet people end up with less of themselves, their families, and nature, in debt, exhausted and unhappy. Where does it all stop?

This book helps you to stop and create simple self-caring, calming moments for *you*. Sometimes just stopping for a cup of tea, to enjoy some undemanding stretches, or to drink a glass of water can be comforting and relaxing. You and those you love will find ten to sixty-second ideas here, which can be used easily throughout your day. Gently and powerfully, you'll dissolve aches, pains, tension, and even arguments. There are also easy to read instantly achievable ideas to help you get out of your seat and take more precious moments in nature! In the evenings, you can relax with heart-touching stories and soothing photos.

Even if your workdays are long but your evenings short, taking moments of self-care will make you happier, calmer, and will improve your life. When you feel the need to uplift or nourish, give yourself the moments you deserve right now and any time you want them. You will thank yourself!

You are Beautiful

This is a chapter about self-love ... self-honor.

We each have a unique background, culture, and life history, with diverse strengths and gifts, and our own special way of expressing love. No one's love is greater or lesser. We've all experienced similar hurts, challenges, and vulnerabilities in this wonderful world.

Getting to know yourself is one of the most loving things you can take time to do. Listen less to others and more to what you and your most loving inner world say to you.

Remember you.
If you are not giving yourself the time and care that you deserve,
How will others be able to figure out how to approach you and give you kindness or care?
For that matter,
How can you give the kind of care you want to give to others,
If you are not first filled with it yourself?
—Marilyn Idle

Like Each Star in the Universe You Are Unique

The best days of my life arrived when I really listened to myself. That is when I learned about me and my preferences—who I really am—not who well-meaning others said I was, could be, or wanted me to be. Many years ago if you had asked me, "Who are you?" it is possible I would have told you what family I was from, what school I went to, or something about what others wanted me to be.

I have had too much input from others and not enough from me. I've been influenced by formal educational institutions (twenty-one years in all), well-meaning, single-viewed, non-holistic medicalized "healthcare" providers, and by imbalanced profit-dominated corporate news and television with its stacked coverage that instigates feelings of personal and mass helplessness, emptiness, longing, sickness, tragedy or horror—which, apparently, is very good for sales and profit. I got input from improve-yourself-buy-more-stuff magazines, entertainment guidance from extreme Hollywood "role models," and well-meaning, yet soul-pinching ideas from several of the "correct" religions.

Yet now, I ask, how is it that so many paths in this world appear to misdirect us away from the simplicity of a direct connection to self and love? After all my time on Earth, having never had enough time or focus directed toward learning about unique *me*, I finally gave myself the love I'd always wanted. I invite you to listen and learn from the best friend of all: your self-loving *you*.

Listening to Yourself: Your Life Has Only the Meaning You Give It

I immediately noticed that listening to myself made me happier. You know yourself and your life better than anyone else. If you aren't already doing so, stop and listen to what you think and feel. Do it often each day and it will help you make happier, more adventurous life choices, your way, on your say. Before you make decisions, ask yourself: Is this really good for me, good for nature, and good for life on our planet?

Your Life is Your Sacred Story

As hard or easy as your life has been, it is your life. When you look back on it each night, remember, this is your one and only precious self. Hopefully, you will share your life story from time to time with loving others and they will share theirs with you. Some people you meet along the way may not have learned how to safely share sacred life stories with mutual respect. Maybe they don't know how to listen with love and patience, or they just can't relate to where you have been on your life journey—especially if your story has been quite painful, scary or rocky. If so, love them. An understanding smile can be enough. When it feels right, share your tales, talk and listen. Many people in this technological day and age are lonely for real sharing. It doesn't cost a thing. Sharing your humanity with another person is so important because it's part of the bittersweet fun of living on this crazy planet, where (apparently) none of us get to take our material techno-things with us, or leave "physically" alive. Life is more fun when you share your hugs, jokes, foibles, vents, whimsies, and wisdom, face to face. Do that each day because life is short. At your funeral, when your less than one-hundred-year life is over, your loved ones will be able to tell your stories because they heard them from you!

Today, if you ask who I am, I'd say two things: I am *pure love* just the same as *you*. My answer to every one of your questions would be what comes to my lips in that moment of being with you

and you with me. If you were sitting next to me, I would be inspired simply by having you, another radiant star in the universe, shining in your own way beside me.

You are the Wise or Sacred One for You

For the longest time, I looked for the wise or sacred one. I found there are too many gurus, experts, and teachers, with too many rules (for me) to follow. If I'm talking with another human being and they don't stop at some point, take a breath, and send me back to wise, sacred *me* for my humble input too—I don't follow them very far down the road.

If Others Try to Run My Life

It feels good to think and feel, to have your own preferences and opinions, and to be in charge of your life. (Take a refreshing breath!) What do you think? When others try to run my life, I offer respect where respect is due—if they are fully informed. Then gently, lovingly, powerfully, and sometimes laughing very loud, I say, "Hold it! I'm in charge of me, and I hold views, sometimes, that are very different than yours. So, I will run me and you can run you. Growing separately yet together in this world, we can be free and each a self-honoring *me*."

Your Beautiful Body

How much do you know about the way your body functions? With simple bodily understandings, you can be fully empowered to do healthy things for yourself that support your body daily. Your interconnected cells, tissues, nerves, organs, cleansing systems, and bones will love you for becoming more self-aware! You don't have to blindly rely only on expensive medical experts and scientists, unless you require or desire them. Instead, find within this book or in your own research, answers to your questions and build self-empowered, self-care in which you nourish, cleanse, calm, rest, and heal your one-of-a-kind body!

It is so easy to learn about how your body works. I learned so much by reading an eighth grade science textbook. Did you know that one quart of water passes though your kidneys every minute! Get to know a little more about your body's organs and systems every day! It's easy and fun to learn about being well and staying well, and it is *not* as complicated as a system which proffers more fixes and pharmaceuticals as by focusing mainly on detecting, aggressively fighting or managing disease rather than supporting health. Did you know that when you get about six ounces of liquid in your bladder, a mechanism signals you that you have to go to the bathroom … and if you put off going, at about eighteen ounces your pants will be wet? Learn more about you. You are fascinating.

Preventive Care Brings Personal Power

If you desire to have fewer life threatening diseases requiring dramatic, extremely costly, heroic interventions like drugs, surgeries, implants, or transplants, you can learn to prevent problems and create health daily. You can have peace of mind by building your personal inner ways of knowing about and healing your body. How? Jump on the Internet; read some books or wellness magazines. Yet, the most important thing in preventing costly problems is listening daily in quiet moments to your own precious body and giving it the rest and re-energizing (big breath) and care it needs!

Too Tired to Even Think? Then Don't!

Have you ever been so tired you can't even think? (Lucky you, if you haven't!) In today's fast-paced world, take a moment, get away from daily routines, and rest yourself. Breathe, calm and relax your mind.

As a child, I remember walking by a peaceful wishing-well full of fish and tadpoles swimming in it. On my way home, after too much of the boxed-in, on-paper, mental work of school, I was often too tired to even think. I'd stop, and with the sun beaming down on me I'd sit by the pond and watch the goldfish swim.

If you are too tired to think, take this moment to breathe, soothe, and rest. Free your mind of the chatter of the day in solitude or with others.

Some advice from a Spanish proverb: "How sweet it is to do nothing and then to rest afterward."

Quiet Time to Think and Feel

Wearing a navy business suit and high heels, I ran out of the courthouse one day, grabbed some fast food, sat on a concrete bench in highly polluted air near a highly polluted lake, in a car-jammed city where I worked—and quickly ate.

Something was concerning me that day, in fact, there were one hundred "somethings" concerning me. Yet, I was too numb and too busy to know what the things were. Then, as I walked across the pavement, my eyes fell on a few green flowering bushes, some small trees, leaves flicking in the breeze, and a garden in the middle of all the concrete and rush.

I walked past the garden and then stopped. I couldn't move. I looked down and saw that I was standing on a metal plaque. I read the plaque and it said "Peace Garden." My tired heart pounded, my head and body tingled and like an unexpected pouring rain, tears fell from my eyes.

On that day something changed in me. If there are one hundred "somethings" concerning you, in a world that feels crazy, I invite you to stop and take some quiet time in your "peace garden."

Is There Something You Say About Yourself That Puts You Down?

I can't begin to count how many times I have heard people (and I used to be one) berate and put

themselves down when they make a mistake. If this is you, how does it help to dump a pail of insults on your head when you already feel terrible about making a mistake? It doesn't help. If, after you spill something, you say "I'm clumsy," or after stepping on a toe, "I can't dance," or after losing a game, "I suck at this game," or after experiencing a failed relationship, "it's the story of my life, unlucky in love," or after putting your foot in your mouth, "I'm no good with people," then *stop it*! The next time one of these unhelpful thoughts comes up, breathe and ask yourself this: "Who might I become if I simply delete these put down words and start over with self love and care?"

12

Wonderful, Different You, Loving Those You Love

Someone in my family once told me, "You are different than us; you must have been found in a cabbage patch." At the time, I took that as a compliment because somehow I knew it was good to be different. Yet, on another level, it also hurt. Being part of a family can be wonderful and at other times can be like being one cog in the larger family machine, instead of a whole, unique, and evolving person. Even while you're part of your family, you're a separate and unique *you*, and you are lovable and belong just the same. You don't have to lose one bit of beautiful you in order to also be part of a healthy, happy family.

Are You Along for the Ride in Someone Else's Life?

You don't have to be a passive passenger in another person's life, whether they're at work, home, or in your community—especially if their life feels like a never-stopping train to you. Take turns being the driver. Unless you *like* being a passive supporter of someone else's plan. And some people do. If that is you, there is nothing wrong at all if you are happy and fulfilled. But, if you don't want to just follow or be pushed along, become a creative co-navigator.

Do You Shrink When You're Told You're Different?

If this has happened for you, you may hesitate to be yourself or express your feelings or thoughts since you feel you might not fit in or might rock others' boats. You are an individual in a relation-ship! In this big universal ocean of life, there is enough room for everyone to be and express who they are, and everyone makes waves. Never stop being and expressing yourself. Even if some days that causes you to be considered wrong, unpopular, scrutinized, ignored, misunderstood, or sometimes even rejected. So what? Those things happen even when you don't express yourself or make waves!

People in healthy relationships can be different and express their views. That is how new understandings come about each day. Be different. Stand up and express yourself, especially in the roughest moments, because if you don't who will? There is no better person to make "your waves" in this world than you, so keep being and expressing different wonderful you!

You Are Loved

I have heard people say that love hurts. Yet what may be true is that love actually dissolves hurt. Try saying "I love both of us" to someone, especially if you are both angry and feeling hurt. See what happens. Also, find out what happens when you say quietly within, "I love myself."

13

Self-care by Night and Day

This is a chapter to remind you to motivate yourself daily to consider your unique life and find and use your favorite self-care tips.

I ran upstairs to the media room to check on homework and music practice with our son: not his favorite conversation, and I was feeling tired. Based on past experience the situation was destined to be uncomfortable for us both. However, I listened to how my back was feeling before I spoke. To my son's surprise, I lay down on the floor and placed my feet on the wooden arm of the futon. I quietly did a few gentle stretches for my back. He looked at me quizzically and asked what I was doing. I replied I was checking on his homework and music plans.

Instead of a getting into a heady conversation, he searched for a song and musical score on his computer and invited me to listen as he played it with YouTube through his speakers and then printed off the sheet music. This was the first song he had ever chosen to learn. Normally, he let his music teacher tell him what to do. Tears came to my eyes. I said, "Are you planning to learn to play that beautiful song on the piano?" He nodded. We were both tired after a long day. From my moving to the floor and caring for my aching body *first*, we both relaxed. Then, from a different calm caring place we easily helped and understood each other.

Touching, because I took him to piano lessons starting when he was four years old but he never wanted to play. I wanted to bring music into his life so that it could be a forever-friend to him. For ten years he told me that I was mean and that if not "forced" he would quit. He said he hated it and that it was ruining his life. And then, this gentle new self-step happened.

Many people push themselves hard during their day at work then give so much to relationships and family concerns that they become exhausted, with little time left for themselves.
If this is the case for you it is important to take in some tender moments. Throughout this book are many ways, in as little as sixty seconds, to have powerful moments of caring self-attention. I believe you and your family will love them so I happily invite you to do them.

Give Yourself Care Often

If I neglect to take three to ten minutes for myself when I need to think about something, or to comfort or soothe, to fill myself up or to calm down, I notice deep tiredness or pain can build over time. I end up feeling off-color and depleted, having to take days or even a week for down time. I may also begin looking outward for something or someone to blame for my lack of self-awareness, neglect, or suffering, and that's not fair or healthy.

When I become self-absorbed or self-obsessed, I now recognize that I've been neglecting self-tending! Now, hands down, I choose self-care versus self-sacrifice, self-obsession, self-absorption, or unfairly lashing out at others. If you desire more care, *stop*, go within, refill, nourish, read about a new skill, exercise, eat well, or do one stretch, even if it is for only a couple of minutes every hour!

What Do I Need?

One hard-working man I spoke to actually said he would be dead before he could be stress-free or able to rest. I have met people (I used to be one of them) who put off giving themselves care until they literally drop. Many people wait until the end of the day, the weekend, or even until the holidays to nourish! "Waiting until later" allows tension and/or injury to build, which could hurt you, your body, or your relationships. In addition, if you don't stop in your busy day to make yourself comfortable or to take a deep breath, you can even become numb, empty, and exhausted, and this can affect your overall enthusiasm for life.

If you are new to the concept of being good to *you*, one simple way to begin is to stop three times during your day and quietly sit back. Rest your hands on your thighs, become focused on your heartbeat and listen to it for sixty seconds. After you learn some quick one-minute rest-stop ideas, start doing them several times during your day, every day for the rest of your life.

If you think you may forget about you and let stress build up, put up sticky notes with the word *Care* written on them. Every time you pour yourself a glass of water, have a salad, stretch your arms, take a deep breath, or go outside for some air or anything else, remove a sticky note and pat yourself on your (much more relaxed) shoulder!

The Energy of Feelings

We all have them, feelings, that is (emotion). We express our experiences through laughter, tears, singing, yelling, quiet thoughts, or anger as we respond to the ups and downs of life. Some years ago, I discovered what much of the Eastern side of the world has always known: that emotion is also energy. Take the word emotion and look at it like this:

NOTE:

CARE

~ for me

15

e-motion = energy in motion. This energy comes from you, yet is also drawn from the Earth and universe. Where your feelings go, energy flows, so it is helpful for you to learn healthy ways to know, express, and enjoy your wonderful energy.

If your feelings get bottled up or difficult to express, they can become compacted into tight balls of energy and experienced as either rage or depression. This can cause hopelessness or other physical and mental stress-related "dis-eases." Two hundred and thirty million prescriptions of antidepressant drugs are written annually in the US for depression, yet recently I saw a commercial touting that if your prescription isn't working they have another drug you can take with it! Currently they are testing antidepressants on seven year olds! Where does it stop?

If you think some of your feelings are blocked, then every hour and every day ask your beautiful heart, which beats forever for you, "What is the feeling or energy I need to safely express?" Hear the messages from your heartbeat and allow your feelings to flow in safety, lowering your stress, and if you desire, bringing drug-free ideas for wellness and ease into your life.

Fill that "Hungry Feeling" with Self-Care

Here's why you may not feel fulfilled, sometimes, by what you eat: You may not realize that what you really want is emotional or *soul* food! When those hungers come up, ask yourself this: "What might nourish my feelings, emotional heart, spirit, or soul?" Here are some ideas to get you started:

- Find a comforting read or write some caring words of your own
- Give yourself a home spa facial
- Do a self-massage on your shoulders, neck, feet or hands
- Rest, stretch, or other self-care
- Do some gentle push-ups against a wall or stairs
- Pick up some scented candles or enjoy aromatic smells
- Make a small drawing of something from nature

- Wrap your arms around you and have a strong, relaxing, self-hug
- Learn the words to a song, hum to your heartbeat or tap or play music
- Dance or do something you've never done before for fun
- Have a sea salt or bubble bath
- Roll down a grassy hill and be in the arms of nature

Give yourself these soulful "foods" often. I believe it is possible that the reason many people survive in places where they may have little to eat is that they find ways to be soothed, self-comforted, or inspired to carry on with the energies of nature—emotional soul foods.

Stop for Just a Moment

Many people have become so busy, it seems to me, they begin to act more like programmed machines than people (this used to be me!). If you are like a robot, seemingly with no human needs, and you've lost your instinct to play, have fun, or rest, I urge you to stop during your day every sixty minutes for sixty seconds to breathe calmly, deeply, and slowly, resting quietly for a moment. Each time you stop and give yourself any amount of care you dissolve pain and tension from your body and refill with energy. These little moments during the day will leave enough joie de vive (joy of life) left in you, so you can have fun later, on your own or with those you love!

Drink in Care and Healing from Water

Like rain to the Earth's bodies of water, your body's inner ocean needs refreshing and refilling regularly. Sluggishness, aches, and *dis-ease* caused by dehydration can be prevented and relieved by remembering to drink water or eat water-loaded plants or foods.

Water has many roles throughout the body, including flushing your kidneys of acidic waste. It dissolves minerals, acts as part of your nutrient delivery system, lubricates, hydrates, and regulates temperature. If you forget to drink enough water over a very short time this can lead to headaches, lethargy, and mental confusion, and increase the risk of constipation, urinary tract infections, and kidney stones. Enjoy some pure water! If your water is chlorinated, filter it or pour some water into a glass or jug and let it stand on your counter or in the fridge for a few hours: the chlorine will dissipate into the air.

If you feel heated, inflamed, arthritic, easy to anger, irritated, are having difficulty concentrating, have dry skin or lips, joint pain or stiffness, or simply feel tired, water could be what you need. If, like me, you are not a water guzzler (yet) and if you often reach first for juices, tea, coffee, soda, wine or beer, choose to drink an ounce (or more) of pure water before you have the other.

Every glass of water you drink refreshes and nourishes you. Naturally, you give it back to the ground waters, plants, trees, soil and insects. It becomes mist and clouds and then rains down from the airways fit for birds, animals, the fish and for people to drink again. Drink pure water and keep yourself balanced so when you give it back, with nature's help, it becomes pure and you can once again drink and enjoy it.

What Is It That I Don't Prefer Today?

If no one has yet asked your opinion, what you think, or what you do or don't prefer today, go within and ask yourself! It's a good thing to do from time to time. Check "in" throughout your day, even when others may not ask for your opinion or input. Asking within is self-kindness. It values and cares for you. If you are not sure where you stand or what you do prefer, you can start by at least asking yourself, "What *don't* I prefer?"

Caring for Wonderful Whole You

One hundred percent of the time now, I see myself as a whole person with a mind and heart, who is evolving and valued. Years ago, during a break from work, I'd enjoy a short enjoyable read from one of my favorite magazines. Yet now, I cringe when I see the pharmaceutical and fix-you ads, which say, "You need drugs" and "You are not OK" or "You are a broken person who needs to be put back together *our* way!" You are *not* a cluster of separate unrelated wrong or broken parts to be fixed with makeup and surgery tricks; nor are you a target to be groomed to take a growing list of expensive drugs for the latest new illness.

There was a time when I was tripped up by these promotions asking, "What is wrong with you?" and I constantly looked for what it might be. Now I focus on sources of information who respect me as perfectly fine.

Long Ago How Did We Heal?

I feel humbled by thoughtful, skilled doctors who educate, motivate and inspire their patients in self-care. These wonderful physicians encourage lifestyles that advance wellness. They prescribe relaxation, stress release, exercise, nutrition, and simple natural remedies. They offer medical options while advocating self-empowering informed choice.

I know people who run to a drug-prescribing doctor for almost every pain. They are constantly worried about getting a disease and dying. How stressful this must be! Yet, I understand this because there was a time when I was influenced by the sickness business and had very little self-knowledge. I didn't know that I could heal almost 100% of the time, naturally, on my own, and without a doctor prescribing a drug! Now I have learned about the principle of balance and I heal myself every day using it.

What did our ancestors do to heal themselves before doctors, drugs, chiropractors, and hospitals were available to help with an imbalance or injury? Though they felt pain and often even terror, they self-stabilized by calming themselves within. Step-by-step, with the help of nature and nurture, they healed themselves. What didn't kill them made them stronger and wiser! You and I can also more consciously use the powerful natural healing forces within us to help us repair, re-energize and regenerate daily.

I love knowing that in case of an unexpected traumatic injury, wonderful paramedics, ambulance drivers, emergency doctors, chiropractors, and hospitals are there to help! Yet, I never forget that the ultimate repairer, re-energizer, and regenerator who works with others on my "wellness team" is self-healing me!

You are the one who heals your body—in all cases—no matter what kind of injury you have, or what kind of assistance you may choose. Remember who you are; know that your highest most loving wisdom from within can calm your body, stabilize your emotional energy, and move you through pain. You can hold your *own* hand, no matter how long it takes, until you are well again!

Do a Self-Care Body Scan

Here is a preventative wellness self-care body scan in which you review yourself and body daily or before going to sleep at night, with your mind's eye, using no machines, no technicians and no technology! Millions of dollars are now spent on medical scanning devices to detect diseases, yet I have met few doctors who ask, "What do *you* think you need to be well?" As the bridges between self-empowered preventative wellness and traditional trauma care are being built, here is a way to increase your own bodily self-awareness. The self-scan is easy, quick, revealing, and fun to do. You can scan yourself to detect energy blocks and even prevent imbalances, as your body will "report" the areas of tightness, pain, or numbness, which need care, nourishment, release, relaxation, regeneration or re-energizing. Here's how to do it:

- Stand, sit, or lie down (you can do this self-scan in short order any time during the day or night). Breathe and gently tune in to your body.
- Bring your attention to your head, or if you prefer, start at your feet. Slowly travel in your mind's eye to each tight, restricted, achy, or painful area of your body (just by doing this, you may feel tingling and life energy circulating in your body).
- For stubborn areas, which remain tight or stiff, a fun way to relax after you scan is to envision a beautiful color washing over the area, releasing, softening, comforting, or soothing. Breathing normally, gently lay your hands on achy areas just as you would to comfort a child who is hurt.
- If simply scanning with self-attention has not encouraged tension to release or energized you, your body may have a *request*: it may be to rest, play, or nourish yourself more often each day. Listen to it! If you're at work, do some sixty-second quick fixes or stretches three to six times in your day, and then plan when at home to rest or play even more!

Here are some more ideas you can ponder to help you re-balance as you self-scan:

- Have I been ingesting low nutrient, low energy food, empty sugary drinks, coffee, or too much alcohol, making my body chemistry acidic, hot, and inflamed, and starving my cells of oxygen?
- Have I been hurting myself with bothersome, unhelpful put-down thoughts?
- Am I stressed by unresolved concerns, whirling around, pressing to be dealt with? If so, calmly, jot them down.
- Have I been overworking, neglecting to flow, change positions, or get up and move about from time to time?
- Am I taking enough peace, comfort, self-protection, or rejuvenation time?
- Am I listening to and acting on my personal dreams and goals daily?

Don't be surprised if your peaceful inward attention and care not only helps your body, mind and emotions to be well, but also soothes your spirit and soul!

When It's Hard to Let Go of Deeper Hurts

A special note about what I call *great injury*: For many people, cellular memories from serious traumatic injuries or feelings—ungrieved losses, which can even be physically painful—come up during a self-scan. When these come up, remember you are now safe and comforted, so you *can* relax, let go of long held pain or tension, and heal more deeply.

Your attention, love and self-care can free your energy at a very deep level where it may have become blocked. Your inner wisdom knows when you are strong and wise enough to handle these deeper releases in safety. You are finding your way to everything you need to be whole, healed, well, and happy now.

Tapping Into Your Inner Wisdom

Your most loving inner wisdom can help you care for yourself because it can go beyond what you have been taught or what you think and feel. Your inner wisdom is the pure love part of you—it *is* you—the helpful quiet voice or feeling that only helps and never shames, dishonors, or harms you!

Anyone can tap into this wisdom, yet trusting it is another thing! If you were influenced (and who wasn't) by this crazy culture's often imbalanced way of looking outside and trusting the "wisdom" of others, you may not be used to listening within. You might ask (as I once did): "How am I supposed to figure out which voice is this deeper, self-loving wise part of me?" The key is to listen to your quiet loving answers to your own questions, and try out only the ones that respect, love and honor you!

Wonderful You

If you are new to self-care and are looking at your body, feeling nervous about what you may find out about yourself, remember to always look through the eyes of love and gentleness. Resolve not to look for what's wrong with you, but for what is right and well with you!

And, as you grow and change each day, even if you find lumps or bumps in your body, fearlessly learn about you and what you need to be well. As you experience your lumps, bumps, and humps along this journey called life (as we all regularly do), don't panic. You, your life, and your body change all of the time, very similar to the Earth's changing weather and seasons! Even if you do discover a problem in your body's landscape, *do not* think "Omigosh ... disease!" Instead, ask and listen to all the loving possible answers to your question: "What do I need to discover next to be well, nourished, and cared for?"

When you look at yourself in a mirror in the morning, don't judge or worry about what you find. Love you. Don't compare with the latest best shape or appearance fad. How does that help you get to love, know, and celebrate unique you? It doesn't. This the-same-is-good mentality leaves out much of who you are. If a trend inspires you, teaches you about yourself, or makes you happy, then go for it! Otherwise, let it go!

Make Deep Self-Connection with the 3-6-9 Dolphin Breath

Sometimes, during a stressful day, you may find you are breathing shallowly. Whenever you need more oxygen, feel stressed or anxious, do this 3-6-9 Dolphin Breath. It's a very simple way to relax and care for your body without drugs or any negative side effects. In order to fully oxygenate your lungs and body:

Lie down, sit on a chair (or stand up straight) and put your chin to your chest and make your neck long. Imagine "a ribbon" rising from your heart and gliding up through the top of your head, lifting you gently up.

Place the tip of your tongue softy up against the back of your front teeth as you breathe in silently through your nose to the count of 1, 2 and 3. Hold your breath to the count of 4, 5 and 6. Then purse your lips and exhale through your mouth to the count of 7, 8 and 9, making a wonderful audible "phwooh" sound like sound a dolphin or whale makes from its blowhole. That completes one full 3-6-9 Dolphin Breath.

Do a total of three. (Hey, that's nine seconds per breath, twenty-seven seconds to care. That's only thirty seconds ... three seconds to spare!) To help yourself to remember to do this, at first you may want to do a 3-6-9 Dolphin Breath before you rise in the morning, in the shower or before you sleep at night.

When you do this simple breath daily you support your body ocean in many impressive ways:

- This breath increases your energy by rebuilding your subtle *chi* or life energy system
- It improves blood flow and cleansing in the circulatory system
- It enhances cell oxygenation throughout your body
- The increased oxygen intake with every breath revitalizes your respiratory system, reducing mental and physical fatigue
- Calms and bathes the nervous system
- Acts as a pump to massage internal organs and improve digestion
- Relaxes and balances the endocrine and hormone systems
- The action on your diaphragm pushes lymph throughout the body, supporting cleansing by helping to eliminate toxic wastes, strengthening your immune system

- Refreshes the eliminatory systems by helping to flush fluids and massage your kidneys and intestines
- Makes your skin more radiant through improved blood flow, oxygenation, and by decreasing the workload of eliminating metabolic wastes, since doing this breath releases them directly and immediately through exhalation.

If you feel inclined, try another breath and feel the calm, right now:

Breathe in through your nose 1, 2 and 3,
Hold your breath for 4, 5, and 6, and
"Phwoosh" let go through pursed lips 7, 8, and 9.

Ways of Boosting Your Energy

We all do it … overexert. If you are like me, you may put in an extra few hours of work by drinking a pot of coffee and eating chocolate to help you forge through. However, if you have a lot of extra work to do, and are already exhausted or worn-out, none of these temporary perk-you-up boosts will be helpful or good for you.

If you know that you have a stressful time in your life coming up such as a late night at work, a household move, a wedding, a trip or a change in your family life or at work, get to bed seven to ten minutes earlier than usual. Use that time to do a self-massage. You can find simple ways to do that described later in this book. This special time for you can support a deep and relaxed sleep before the stressful day arrives.

Use these common sense ideas to rebuild your energy, de-stress and relax during a stressful day:

- Stop several times during a hectic day and take ten seconds to breathe deeply.
- Prevent a build-up of tension and aches and refill your energy by twice in your day lying down for three wonderful relaxing minutes.
- Fake a yawn and for ten seconds stretch out and wiggle your back, neck, arms and legs.
- Sneak away for three to ten selfish minutes and snuggle into a comfy sofa. Close your eyes and wrap a soft comforter or your arms around you for a self-hug.
- Anytime you need to, stop what you are doing and relax.
- Crunch nutritious raw food like carrot, celery or cucumber sticks or grab a few grapes or sliced apple or pear. Eat a handful of raw nuts or seeds as they are filled with essential brain and nerve-nourishing fats.
- Bank some extra energy before and during a stressful time by zipping out for a very short brisk three minute walk or run. Do this every hour as breathing fresh air will increase your circulation and improve your body's ability to transfer oxygen to cells.
- Drink de-caffeinated coffee or at least half regular and half de-caf. Coffee has the ability to provide a rush of energy yet activates your stress hormones. Too much caffeine in any form can cause adrenal stress and energy burnout! So, try to avoid excesses of tea and coffee.

If I am working late I like to drink a small glass of lemon water in between each cup of coffee or tea. Or I may add half a cup of milk or milk alternative to my coffee or tea to make it into a more nutritious latté. Avoid "energy" drinks because they may not bring any real nourishment and instead stimulate a jittery amped-up false sense of energy. If you have to work late or finish a project, switch over to healthier drinks like juices and super-food green shakes, made with fresh fruits and vegetables, which do nourish you and enhance your energy.

Tips for a Good Night's Sleep

A soothing comfortable technology-free bedroom encourages sleep. Here are some ideas to get you started.

- Make sure your bedroom is as dark and noise free as possible.
- Turn lights down thirty minutes before sleep as the presence of light can interfere with your body's preparation for sleep.
- Even if you feel extremely tired in the daytime, make sure to nap for no more than thirty minutes.
- Avoid alcohol for a few hours before going to bed and don't smoke, chew nicotine gum or have caffeine in the later hours of the day as these can make it hard to fall asleep.
- Treat yourself to little exercise spurts during the day to prevent a build-up of body tension or sleep disturbing aches and pains. Run up and down the stairs, do push-ups against the wall, do three sit-ups or thirty seconds of running on the spot. Small bouts of these activities, even at night, can help shake out muscle tension, de-stress and help you have a peaceful sleep.
- Make sure that you receive sufficient iron from the foods you eat especially if you are a woman or if you work a lot near technology, as iron deficiency can lead to disturbed sleep or even lack of sleep.
- Make your bed and bedding comfortable as a hot, not-so-comfy, hard or lumpy pillow might cause a disturbed sleep.
- For ten minutes before going to bed invite yourself to: take three deep breaths and relax, listen to some quiet soothing music, take a warm bath or do a few yawns and stretches. If you still need to wind down, put the kettle on to boil, then sip a cup of herbal tea. All this is sure *to* tempt sleep. (I'm feeling more relaxed and drowsy just writing this!)

Where Thoughts Go Energy Flows

This is a chapter about paying attention to what you are thinking about during your day and the effects on self, relationship or life.

Whatever you are thinking right now, take a second and scrutinize it! Is it helping you move toward what you desire? Or is it adding unintended thought-force to conditions in your life that you don't want?

Your thoughts are subtle energy. They create amazing circumstances. In your personal or work-life, your views and words, when acted upon again and again, create your relationships and experiences, your life circumstances in this physical world. Therefore, it's well worth looking at what you are thinking, saying, and doing, and whether or not you like the creative results. Maybe there is something *else* you could think about and do, which would make you happier and freer!

Thoughts are Vibrations

I love this energy called *thought*. Thoughts are tiny vibrations and subtle pulses, creative energy similar to any other energy source that you use to create things or circumstances. Every thought has its own ripple effect within you, and the potential to create something outside and around you in your life!

Destiny or Fate

Have you ever wondered why having lots of things or relationships comes so easily to some people, while other people's dreams never come true? Do you feel that your unconscious patterns are your predetermined fate, as past programs automatically play out their unquestioned scripts?

I do not believe in fate or fixed events. Rather, to me, life is what happens as you think about and choose varying paths of thought or action. If you don't like what is before you, think about what you would prefer in your life, about what you believe is possible, and about whether you are at least willing to see if it's possible! Then, act in the direction you want to go. No matter how long it takes, bring something new into the world for you! Don't resign to fate unless you really like your "fate" the way it currently is.

What Are You Thinking About?

Think. Have you ever taken the time to think about what you are thinking about? If you are running on automatic pilot (like I once was), you may find that when you stop and look at the thoughts you dwell on, you are putting way too much energy back into conditions you don't like, such as:

- Not enough money to pay your bills
- Fear about getting hurt, dying, or getting a disease
- Ruminating on how unsatisfying your job, relationship or life is

If you're putting much of your energy into grumbling that is not helping you to create what you really want in your life, stop it. Create balance. Complain a little, maybe ten percent of the time, then put the other ninety into new ideas and actions that will actually move you toward what you prefer for your life (or what you would like to see evolve on this precious Earth).

Watch Only TV Shows That Nourish You (and Cut Out the Mind-Numbing Stuff)

I cut out watching television a long time ago, especially the news, because it left me down, empty, needy, and feeling like something was missing from my life. Now, when I do, very occasionally, join my husband to watch a family show, and those appalling drown-you-with-input-until-you-can't-breathe commercials come on, before it's too late, I holler, "Mute, mute, hit the mute button!" I actually put my hands in front of my eyes during the let's-see-how-we-can-cram-into-your-eyes-and-load-this-into-your-mind commercials.

If you are watching television daily, and if you are not good at ignoring the terrorizing, shocking, distressing, hypnotizing messages, you may be feeding your subconscious mind with disheartening untrue rubbish that you ruminate on throughout your day. If you feel something is wrong with your life after watching TV, something likely is—the stuff on the TV.

Is Thoughtful Self-care the Solution to all the World's Problems?

If you are in touch with yourself and care for you daily, inevitably you will remember to care for the things that allow you to be alive, like the air, water and soils of earth! The air you breathe, the soil you grow plants in, the waterways you drink from—they are all interconnected. If these earth ecologies are healthy, then you can enjoy them and be healthy too. Many people are becoming aware that all avenues: nature's life, your life and business life, such as the processes of creating goods to sell, are also interconnected. Eventually imbalance or harms affect us all. That is why self-care is an important daily step. If you feel well and cared for, then, you remember to respect the earth and to do business in the same caring way.

Quietly in your thoughts (or maybe you will be vocal about your opinions like I am) you can talk from time to time to a young person about your caring ideas. By doing this you will help them in this technological age become understanding of and connected to the airways, waterways, seeds and soils of this beautiful earth. Each time you have an idea about how you can be caring to you—it is likely to help others too. With your quiet calm and clear voice, share it.

There was a time when only a few people, "at the top" it seemed, made decisions which we all had to live with. However that approach does not work as we are seeing. From self to earth care, you, me and everyone has a thought, wisdom, skill, idea or a gift which can help co-existence with nature and each other. Some call this 'peace on earth'. I call it, self-caring, co-peaceable, self-responsible and *sustainable*—living!

> Sometimes your miracle will come together in an instant,
> a few minutes, a few days, a few years, or a few lifetimes
> Nonetheless, all miracles are instant
> if you can see from an infinite perspective.
> —Marilyn Idle

The Observer

I was too busy to observe my thoughts, feelings, and actions, let alone shift them to what I preferred in my life. Hell, I didn't know I didn't prefer what I didn't prefer. I just did what I thought I had to do each day, without much inner observation. Yet, when my life began to weigh me down and I felt unhappy and unwell, I tried positive affirmations! I thought it was all fluff, yet I did notice something: I couldn't feel positive about my day, and that led me to ask myself why. So I observed. You can learn (take a deep breath) to observe, dream, and choose anew in any area of your life. Step by step, quietly, think, feel, act and co-create your life in a new way. Begin by watching what you think, do and talk about. Become aware of what you feel—*or don't feel, if you are hurt or numb*—be the observer if only for sixty seconds now and then during your day!

Laughing Turns on Natural Happiness

This is a chapter about bringing more humor into your day!

It has been said that children laugh one hundred times a day, while adults just laugh ten times a day. No matter how serious our life circumstances can be, no matter what, don't you think it's time to relieve, relax, and find a way to laugh more often? Laughing a hundred times a day may not erase a rough life or challenging circumstances, but it can bring us more uplifting and fun moments.

I think cosmic humor would be a great new spiritual path or religion if we needed one. It might bring in a view that helps everyone make more sense of the sometimes crazy experiences of this world!

If we rarely laugh, it may mean we have settled into viewing only the next inevitable or difficult challenges. This makes life a serious situation! Yet, if we bring in a new view with humor, bouncing over the rough and tumble parts can be more balanced, colorful, and happy too.

We don't need to laugh or be mirthful all of the time, nor do we need to be so serious. Our five senses may be enough for surviving, but for really living I think we need a sense of humor. Life will be so different if we laugh one hundred times a day.

Laughter triggers a gush of beneficial physical and emotional changes and disarms tension and stress. Even expecting jovial laughter before watching a funny movie has neuroendocrine effects. A good laugh is enough to increase the levels of feel-good hormones in your blood! Best of all, this priceless medicine is free, fun, and painless to use.

We need humor in friendship and it can't hurt when meeting strangers or enemies. Humor is infectious, yet sometimes it is great as an internal view or self-dialogue.

The Sound of Laughter Draws Our Attention

If we choose—fun can be more contagious than any complaint or sneeze. When laughter is inclusive it connects people in camaraderie. At home in family or in your coupleship it increases moments of happiness and healthy closeness. If all else fails to satisfy you, find something funny to watch, say, or do. It is a powerful answer to tiredness, stress, pain, and conflict.

Can you think of anything that works faster or more reliably to bring your mind and body or relating back into balance than a good chuckle? Seeing the funny side of life, where you might otherwise have to cry if you didn't laugh, lightens your day. Funny stuff soothes loss or hurts, it inspires good spirits, connects you to your own most loving self and to loving others. With so much power to heal, the ability to laugh helps keeps you grounded, focused on what matters and attentive to building new and better moments.

Remember to express amusement, chuckle, hoot, chortle, giggle, titter and laugh. A joyful outburst is not the worst thing you could do to draw attention and you may by chance cause a person who is having a bad day, to smile.

Developing Your Sense of Humor: Take This Very Seriously (Just Kidding)

I am no stiff-upper-lipped stuffed shirt killjoy, but the direction of my life path made me a person who was a late humor-bloomer. I used to take everything with deathly seriousness and rarely laughed at anything. Been there done that. No fun there! Yet now I do see fun and laughter almost every day even during sad times and even on days or occasions, which are not conducive for laughter. There are many levels. Even during events of great sadness there will be room for heartening or some level of lightening up. There will be a respectful mid-zone where you can decide whether bringing in some cheer is the right thing to do.

See the Funny Side of Life

Laugh at yourself when you can. Instead of being embarrassed by a klutz moment (as long as you and everyone are free of hurt), laugh at it. Attempt to laugh at a bad situation and at the satire and ridiculousness of life situations rather than moan and groan or whine about them. (Okay, whine just a bit, which can be very funny to watch.) When you find yourself facing what seems to be a horrible problem, ask these questions:

Is it that awful?
Is it really worth getting distressed over?

Is the situation beyond repair?
Is it that significant?
Is it really your drama or dilemma
to deal with?
Is it worth upsetting others?
If yes, get support and deal with it.
If not, hit the delete button, then
the humor button.

Remind Yourself to Lighten Up

Keep a goofy thing-a-ma-bob on
your desk or in your car. (I
personally am looking for one of
the spring-loaded, grass-skirted
dashboard hula girls, to remind me
to dance.) Put up a funny photo in
your office, or photos of you and
your family or friends having fun. If you don't have any funny photos then choose a computer
screensaver that reflects your mood. If you don't want to reflect your mood, say the "I feel like
crap today mood," pick a screensaver that makes you laugh.

Many things in life we don't have power over, predominantly, the conduct of other people. Some
people think that taking the burdens of others (or the world) on your shoulders is a praiseworthy
cause. I believe living your own life well and being a role model for the things you value is better.
In the long run, trying to change other people's behavior is impractical, unproductive, bad for
you, and even bigheaded. Take care of your own good life. Keep a whole-view perspective when
deciding whom you will hang out with and share your time and energy with. And don't sweat
over or judge another person's life choices—each to his or her own. Their freedom and fun ends
where yours begins, and hopefully, the two worlds will humorously meet.

Use Good Humor to Overcome Challenges and Perk Up Your Life

Life brings conflicts that can
either get you down or
become playthings for your
imagination. The ability to
laugh, play, and have fun
with others not only makes
life more fun it also helps
you co-solve problems with
others and be more co-
creative of ideas or new life
adventures. So bring
healthy, respectful mirth
into your daily life as it can
renew you, your work, and
all of your relationships.

De-Stress Your Life Daily

Don't focus on other's problems or let your problems pile up. Built up tension or anxiety is unnecessary and a major obstacle to fun, humor and laughter! P.S. Most puppies, kittens, and children are experts on playing, taking life lightly, and being amused or happy. Watch and learn!

Unwind and Be Kind

If you take a problem or yourself too seriously, it can be hard to think. When you get your knickers-in-a-twist or get stuck in dead-end thinking your emotions can get bottled-up, making your compression part of the problem. Instead, breathe and let your passion flow with humor. It may improve inventiveness and speed up finding the solution. Tomorrow is a new day. So get outside the box. Sit on it, and if you lean on your funny bone you may find amusing solutions that please you and others. When you can see a fun side to a problem that is perhaps tender and serious, you can add balance. This often begins to transform a full stop into a minor glitch which is now being solved step by step by creative, fun, and sometimes, even very simple fresh ideas.

Make a Point of Adding More Humor and Play into Your Daily Communications

No matter how bad you are at it (I can well attest to this as I am only learning about humor and being wittier) you can improve the quality of your coupleship as well as your experiences with co-workers, family, and friends. Even if you grew up in a family where laughter wasn't common, you can learn to laugh in your life, in your way. I find the more I invite myself to find the lighter side of life, it can arise naturally in every situation.

When you hear laughter, seek it out and inquire, "What's so funny?" Smile! Consider the absurd, horrible, sad, hurt, and angry things in life as a path back to the good and fun things in your life. Ask those you love, "Have you heard any good jokes or was there anything funny that happened to you today? This week? In your life?" Spend time with amusing, pleasant (older or younger) people who find the humor in everyday events. My son and his friends are amazing at this! They laugh easily both at themselves and at life's absurdities. It is contagious!

Tonight at supper I asked if anyone had heard a good joke lately. (I couldn't tell a joke to save my life.) The table got very quiet. No one had heard a funny yarn lately. Then something really amazing happened. Everything began to have a funny twist to it. I ended up dropping a dollop of potatoes into my glass of red wine. A piece of food jumped up six inches and off one teen's plate as he wasn't looking and tried to put his fork into it. Sometimes if you invite it, even in what seem to be humorless events, life and the universe seem to answer by creating opportunities to laugh!

Playing With Problems Comes Naturally to Children

When they are confused or afraid, some kids make their problems into a game. This gives them a sense of power over and an opportunity to experiment with new "happy ending" scenarios and "save the day" super hero solutions. Going within your imagination or hanging out and interacting in curious or playful ways can

help you keep or breathe life into your precious personal or solution finding abilities.

I have shortened unhappy moments in conflicts by quickly acknowledging the pain, frustration, and difficulty, yet also (if no one was injured or it wasn't a moral or life threatening problem) inviting mutual creative problem solving within exciting laughter and play. See the lighter side of your life and laugh whenever you can. I believe it will take you to a better place within you where you can view your life and the world from a larger perspective that is less stressful and more encouraging, co-creative, happy, and balanced.

Laughter Invites Wellness

Laughter makes you feel good. And the good feeling that you get when you laugh remains with you even after the laughter subsides. Even in the hardest times, when you can muster one, a laugh or even just a smile can go a long way toward making you or others you love feel better.

When sadness, loss, anger, or hurt has been safely dealt with, then having fun or wittiness can shift perspective, allowing you or others to see a painful situation in a different light. Using humor in relationships allows you to be more spontaneous, to let go of judgments or criticisms, and to let emotions safely rise to the surface in a bath of safe respectful laughter.

31

Re-member and Real-ize

This is a chapter about using conscious intention, your thoughts, your feelings and 'life force' to build wellness, yourself and more contented or happier life situations.

There is a pool of limitless cosmic energy connected with the Earth which few people talk about. I call it *neutral life force*. It fuels all creations, no exceptions. Your thoughts, spoken words, written words, intentions, plans, and physical actions put into motion creative energy, so it makes sense to give your attention exclusively to inventing those things and conditions which you really prefer!

This life force, the infinity in the middle of forever, does not judge: There is no good or bad creation, just pure unconditional love for everything! Use your infinite love to consciously co-create everything that you want: no longer will you need to accidentally fuel circumstances that you don't want!

Infinitely Speaking We Love to Love Everything!

You and I are each a wee piece of life *living*. We are infinite love *loving*. We are individuations of *all that is*, human and divine at the same time. Life and love unconditionally fuel all creative urges and circumstances. Everything is fuelled into existence by love and returns to love again and again. Nothing ever leaves the *all*; for a time, we are just in a certain place, in a certain form.

Thoughts on Co-Creating

In this technological era, do not consider yourself alone if you have too many thoughts swirling through your head all day and just want to delete them! So, if you don't want to lose track of good ideas that could be important to you, write them down. That way, you put them out of your mind for the time being. When you're ready to look at them, they'll be there waiting for you.

Keep a "Starlight" Journal

I can't tell you how many times a useful thought to help me co-create my next step comes to me just when I turn out my nightlight to sleep. So, I keep a pen and journal or sticky-note pad by my bed. Many times, I've been certain I'd remember my great idea in the morning, but it always dissolved by then. So now, I take that extra moment to jot things down and this quick act of self-care has been very satisfying. Many times, my next day has gone much better as a result of an insight I scribbled down, slept on, and then paid attention to again during waking hours.

Don't let good ideas pass by to become the classic "twenty-twenty hindsight." We all know it can be upsetting later if you discover you didn't listen to your wisest inner self when it came knocking. I used to ignore mine massively and end up in confusion or turmoil, trusting another's brilliance or inspirational words to tell me what to do, because I ignored my own starlight wisdom! Not anymore.

Thought Energy

Thoughts, words, music, and all forms of energy affect us. A Japanese researcher, Dr. Masaru Emoto, found evidence that human energy expressed by loving or hateful words turned into crystal shapes or discordant lumps after he froze and examined the molecular structure of the ice! He concluded that thoughts of kindness caused beautiful crystalline snowflake patterns to appear, while hurtful, harsh words caused distorted glob-like shapes. Sending loving thoughts to yourself may cause all the water in your body to sparkle with positive life energy.

Setting Intention

Thoughts, then words, are levels of subtle yet influential creative energy. After you think and choose your view, another way to physically manifest what you want is to set a committed intention. You may also want to write up a plan of action. Setting intention takes on quantum power when you use photo images or drawings to build a model on paper of what you desire. The visual image inspires you to step toward your evolving plan of action. It also helps your unconscious to connect with your divine self.

Conscious or Unconscious Creating

Humans create. You are always creating, with or without your thoughtful input. Since you are constantly creating anyway, are you a thoughtful creator, or are you using your energy to fuel someone else's dream or destructive nightmare?

If you are unconscious and not managing your own wee life and connection to infinite potential to think and make clear conscious choices, it is possible you may be letting others use your power! If you're unhappy or hurting, take back control of your own life goals, authority, gifts, and abilities. The happier and more fulfilled you are, the more you have to celebrate and to share with others.

Quantum Intention Using Earth's Fields

Physicists believe there is a quantum field within Earth's plane in which we live and create daily, that affects all waves of possibility in the universe.

As energy, thoughts produce waves. All waves are affected by each other, making new combinations. Some waves increase in their amplitude, while others completely disappear, depending on how they are affected by other waves. Simply put, *your* energy waves affect Earth's quantum co-creative field. There is nothing you can think, feel, or do that does not influence it. Every thought, feeling, and action has its effect in the quantum field, which produces some kind of effect in your life. Therefore, make your waves! Dare to be the one who decides the meaning of your life. Have the courage to be the one who dances into existence what *you* desire to see in your life and on Earth.

Scary Thoughts?

Lately I've noticed that *all* media is heavily weighted with fear-invoking images. Scary thought! I find that if I ignore the thoughts these pictures and words bring with them, most of them dissolve quickly. However, if that doesn't help clear your mind, try this: Every time an unhelpful thought arises, using your mind's eye and your sense of humor, quickly paint a new scene that is happy or funny to replace it with. For example, in my mind's eye, I sometimes decorate my scary thoughts with polka dots!

If terrifying thoughts persist, I unmask them by asking myself what's underneath them (they are now painted in polka dots and looking more and more hilarious). If a fear thought persists, I may go through a reality check to see if I need to prevent a real danger, and if so, create protection or safe haven. But, I don't dwell on scary thoughts because when I ask myself whether they help me or anybody else in any way to be well and happy, the answer I get one hundred percent of the time is *no*.

Once you sort out the imagined from the real potential of scary thoughts, you can arrive at a cleared canvas in your mind to create safe thinking and actions. With your heart now lighter, you can imagine comforting or funny scenarios. No matter how horrible things are or seem, use this potential to create real safety if needed, and then step forward in love and calm.

Venting Angry Feelings

First of all, it is important to recognize that we can all have angry and even destructive thoughts, especially when we feel hurt or frustrated. If you think you don't, you may be repressing feelings that can stress your heart and body. Your anger may be leaking out in hurtful, sneaky or cutting ways that damage your relationships. It's upfront, safe, direct, and productive to *vent* when you are hurt or angry. A vent is a storm or flurry of words that gets out what you're feeling in a safe way. Vents let you blow off words that are not necessarily rational or helpful. They are simply one healthy way to clear the air and get concerns onto the table. Afterwards, you can calm down, take a few big breaths, and find a way to talk in a cooperative and mutually caring way.

Before you start, explain what a safe vent is and that you don't want feedback or a solution in the beginning. Say clearly, "I need to get this out and off my chest first, then find solutions. I will listen to you too." Each person owns their thoughts and feelings one hundred percent. This makes it safe to express strong feelings such as anger, angst, indignation, sadness, rage, frustration, hurt, and so on. Venting is never used to attack. Venting clears the way to rational caring talks and co-solutions. Note: An adult never vents to a child who is too young to understand or use this skill. Don't dump on someone and then stomp away. If a person is scared or unable to listen, stop. Leave only when both people feel respected and problems are co-resolved. If needed, fill up with self or mutual TLC (tender loving care) afterward.

Dark Thoughts of Despair

When you feel dark or despairing, find your way deep into the center of those thoughts—consider them a form of fertile manure—and plant wonderful loving thought-seeds. If it feels like a loving thought couldn't live there, remember the mighty oak tree grows from the tiny brown acorn, and the majestic maple grows from a lime-green key-shaped seed which flies like a helicopter as it drops from the branch!

Imagine a huge green tree or a purple, orange, yellow, red and blue flowering colorful garden growing out of the dark thoughts. See an aqua blue water fountain in the center of a little fishpond and a little playful cat pawing to catch a golden fish. If you perceive scary images shrink them to a tiny creature and wash them with a bright happy color of your liking. Why not? After all these are your thoughts and they only have the meaning and life you give them! Now, the dark thoughts have the company of bright thoughts. It may take years or lifetimes for you to understand what the thoughts were trying to tell you. Meanwhile, you have also created new empowering, wonderful thoughts alongside them to protect, free, and uplift you.

Observe the Impact of Your Words on Others

When you're not thinking kindly about yourself, you're less able to think lovingly toward other people. Take time to carefully choose what you say, especially if you're angry. Will you be kind or unkind, helpful or hurtful? From time to time, take a moment to observe your words carefully to learn their impact. During a conflict, observe how you and other people are affected when you say something like "This is hopeless!" or "You are so wrong!" Then, notice the energy when you say something like "We are both good people, so what can I add here that will help each of us?"

Blueprint

Like a house designer or builder, you can make use of a blueprint. With your intention and a plan to begin, all the forces of the universe can align to help make the impossible possible. Are there dreams or adventures you still want to do? If so, never give up! At the same time, don't just sit there hoping it will happen. (If your goal does spontaneously succeed, more power to you!)

If you want to travel or have a special adventure that seems out of the question due to finances or other reasons, don't let that stop you, even if your knee jerk reaction is to think there's no point. What do you have to lose in planning? If you create a blueprint of what you want to do, first in your thoughts and then on paper, it may lead you to ask questions and take little steps. The thing you want may not happen right away—or maybe it will! You won't know unless you choose what you want to build and create a blueprint.

Naturally Regenerate Your Body: Wellness Thoughts and Intention Can Help

We all ward off thousands of invaders naturally daily as our bodies regenerate, rebuild, and cleanse our cells. However, to speed restoration after injury or strain, your body may need extra help from you with uplifting, loving, wellness thoughts. Examples include: Envision yourself as well; watch comedies and nature shows; see yourself doing playful body movements even as you drag your butt around in your bathrobe.

Also, while you are rebuilding and regenerating with wellness words, ask for and be willing to gracefully receive a little extra help, care, or support. Then, watch as your body systems rebuild and *reboot* because you boosted your self-healing capabilities with your words.

An Interesting Way to Use Your Word-Energy During Dis-ease

When you are sick or injured, in pain or discomfort, like most of us, you may repeat many times over, "I'm sick" or "I'm hurting." There is nothing wrong with saying that. Yet, whether healing at home or with help try adding an empowering thought, something gentle like this: "I am experiencing being sick (or injured), yet, I know somewhere deep within me, my body knows how to be completely well!" Or say, "I am giving myself care to heal right now, but this experience is not all I am: I am well and injury-free."

You have nothing to lose and everything to gain by learning to move your thoughts from one powerful state to another. You are caring for you while you are feeling unwell, and at the same time bridging to *knowing,* in another part of you, that you are also fully whole and perfect. Thus, you invite your energy to both causes.

Thoughts
Images, your life's songs
Feelings, passion
Physically planned for by *writing it down*
Or *directly acting* on your thought
Movement, your dance of life
All personal forces
Universal energy and you acting with it, your way, on Earth
Helping yourself transform your desires
Potential
And your choices
Possibilities
... Into reality.
—Marilyn Idle

Simple Beauty and Comfort in Your Home

This is a chapter about your surroundings and the comfort and care you can create with them.

I like to create beautiful living space wherever I am. Wherever you are, inside or outside, at an office, attending a happy or unhappy gathering, and especially at home, think about how you could make the space around you more refreshing and beautiful.

Take ten to sixty seconds to stop what you are doing and place a pitcher of fresh water (or ocean water if you live near one) into a central spot. Set a plant or flower on a table in your bedroom. Think soothing, comforting thoughts that bring you peace and delight, to your sense of beauty. Everyone will have a different idea of what beauty is. For some it is found in nature: a stone, plant, or piece of driftwood. Others find beauty in placing artwork or pictures of those they love all around. Your thoughtful efforts to bring beauty to your living space strengthen and remind you to be who *you* are.

These acts are your Earthly expression of soulful infinite you. Whatever you decide to place each day around you, take care of these things, polish and refresh them daily. When you desire to change the beauty around you, give back to the Earth those things you will no longer have near you in your living space.

A Simple Candle

Candles are probably as old as the human race, at least since fire was discovered. Candles bring ambiance, a peaceful glow, and they go hand in hand with the word *relax*. Try putting a little drop of essential oil such as lavender or rose in the warm wax of a larger candle. Light a candle and let it remind you to have some peace just for you tonight. Always blow out your candle when you leave the room.

If Your Home Was Your Country

If your home was a small country and you were the leader, would you like to live there? Are you running the special place you call home in a caring way? How thoughtfully tidy are you keeping it? Do you value and repair the old or new resources and polish and refresh the treasures that you keep? Are your plants or pets protected, not endangered species, in your little country due to your attention and care? Is your country cluttered with heaps of toxic or dangerous things that you hoard, do not need, or use? Is your home hospitable, interesting, fun, memorable, and a kind, peaceful, welcoming place to visit? Does it offer safe haven and a soft, comfy place for you and those who visit to relax?

Look over your place of *being* for the next few days or weeks. Decide with fresh eyes, as the leader of your unique place, small or large, old or new, how you desire it to be. Do you want it to stay the same or to become different? If you want to change anything, slowly, over the next few weeks and months, corner by corner, room by room, do it.

If you are one member of a family, you are the watchful leader or an important and valuable co-leader of your place. You, your family, and guests truly deserve this, and your love and care will inspire them to care for and love it too.

Something Special for You

Sometimes something as simple as putting a single flower in a vase or a candle on the table, just for you, can make your world a better place today. What are you going to do to make your world a better place for you today? Breathe and take sixty seconds to think and feel about the simple and wonderful thing that you will do for yourself right now. Then do it now or do it later this evening.

Task Accomplished

Do you have some tasks this day, this week, or this season that feel so mundane, repetitive, hard, or thankless that you struggle with doing them? Tasks, tasks, tasks! If you're like me, after I finish work I'd rather play, visit, or have an adventure, not do more tasks!

We all have to find ways to tackle tasks, some days, when we least want to. Take one step at a time. Do what you need to do step by step, no matter how mundane or hard it may be. When each task is done, ask yourself, "What lovely appreciation and thank you can I give myself today for doing this?"

When You Are Too Tired to Do a Task

There are some tasks that I don't even want to think about doing, let alone do! I know from experience that stating in clear words what I intend to do can help me accomplish a goal. But, what if you are absolutely too tired to think and don't want to plan or intend to do something that you eventually need to do! This happens to many hard working people and if this happens to you, here is a way to get you up and doing a chore you would rather ignore forever:

Let's say you've just *got* to wash those grimy windows because you can't see out of them— before you go to bed, put the window cleaner bottle and paper towels on your kitchen counter; put a sticky note on it targeting one dirty window (just one); then go to bed. To get a large plant re-potted, set the new pot and the potting soil in the middle of your floor on some paper with your soil tools nearby. By the time the roots have grown across your floor to the bag of soil, I'm sure you'll be ready to do it, and your family will be lined up to help, so they don't have to trip over soil, roots, and pot, one more time. To encourage you to make fresh home baking for your child, put the bowl, recipe, and stuff out for three days in a row in plain view. By then, you will have worked up the courage to home bake one plate of cookies with love and patience.

Enjoy just looking at your pots, bowls, window sprayer or whatever task tools you need, sitting about on your counter, or on the floor, at this stage, with no thoughts or pressure. Mobilized-into-action with physical in-your-face intentions, with a bit of luck, you will fall over it and then in a few moments do it, and maybe even enjoy doing it rested, relaxed, motivated, under-whelmed, and maybe even excited!

Carry-On Bags That Create a "Home" For You While Travelling

If you are like me and enjoy traveling, or travel is part of your work, you can create a carry-on mini version of the comforts you love in your own home to take with you. You can do this physically or with your mind's eye. Physically, for example, you can choose clothing that makes you feel good, protected, and soothed like a turtle's shell. Choose your travel clothes for comfort not just looks. Take a little shell or stone from your garden or a special small *objet d'art* to set up in your hotel room. You can "paint" your hotel or meeting room with little things and clothing of colors you like, and you can use your mind's eye to surround yourself with the beautiful color of your soul. Enjoy being soothed and energized in this self-kind way. Happy traveling to you!

Nice Smells

My favorite smells are the air after a fresh rain and clean towels right out of the dryer, or fresh off the line. I love the scent of garden roses. What is your favorite smell—the smell of flowers or the aroma of your favorite delicious food or drink? If you need a simple little perk in your day, add lovely smells! It could be a branch that has broken off a cedar tree, or the rich aroma of organic coffee beans, or some pure vanilla in your kitchen. What nice smells will you find to enjoy for ten to sixty seconds when you need to make you and your nose happy?

Nature Connection

This is a chapter about getting off your chair and going out into nature, even if only for three minutes.

Nature helps me reconnect and be a more peaceful, calm, and free person. I often go outside even if it is only for a moment or two. If you are not touching the natural outdoors as often as you would like, I invite you to. Even a short walk in a park or near some trees can refresh you with the sweet smell of leaves, moss, or soil. You can watch the leaves happily flapping and then realize the same gentle breeze that moves them, whispers near your face.

On one of my walks, a young deer was standing so still a few yards in front of me near a tree that I didn't even notice it until it flicked its white tail up and perkily trotted into the greenery. On another stroll, I felt a soft mist touch my cheek just before a light rainfall began. I learned just how much wildlife pays attention to people when walking near a lake. A gaggle of Canadian Geese stood up and lifted their wings in unison, about to quickly transform into a *skein* (a gaggle in flight). But, they watched to see how many more steps I might take in their direction, and when I stopped and moved quietly backward they all lowered their wings and nestled again into the sun-warmed sand, as their comfort zone was now respected.

Whether you go in solitude or with your children and family or friends, even a few moments can make a huge soothing difference in your day. Every time you come in from a walk you may find that you have remembered more of who you are as a natural person, who brings a bit of the wind in your hair and nature in your heart back into your home or office.

De-Magnetize Your Chair

If you feel almost magnetically stuck to your computer chair or gaming controller, or you've sunk so deep into the sofa in front of your TV that you can barely see above the hole you are in, *stop*. Demagnetize, crawl out, and unplug yourself, if only to prove to yourself that you can. You know you can come right back to your sofa sink hole or magnetic computer chair whenever you desire, so stand up and step away. Put one foot in front of the other and go outside right now, out in nature for one to three minutes or even three to five minutes, or ten minutes, or if you think you can make it, don't go back to technology until tomorrow morning!

Technology Can Draw You Away from Nature: Don't Let It

For many people technology is addictive. If you are one of them (I am) do not let your PC, games, or other devices make you a slave to them or keep you away from nature or those you love. If you focus too much on it, technology can become dehumanizing. It takes away the time you spend being a mother, father, sister, brother, friend, human being, and enjoying the good company of nature, wildlife, and other people. In this short life, it's important to us as humans to experience the beauties of nature and being with others.

Television, DVDs, cellular phones, iPods and the like, are inviting, fun, and out-and-out addictive. I have noticed when several people are using different equipment, the social and face-to-face, hand-to-hand, hug-to-hug, heart-to-heart part of being human can get lost! One day, our son had several friends over and they sat on the futon while one played a video game on the TV screen, another played on the computer, and they all listened to music while using their cellular phones to *text* people who were not in the room. When I find a word to describe my reaction, I will let you know it.

I do have a computer, but I choose not to use wireless or personal pocket-sized devices. The many messaging and music devices that can be attached to you, when used in moderation and balance, can be a great way to be in nature, for example, while jogging with an iPod or connected to those you love by text messaging, yet use precaution if you feel you have been using devices too much. Pull back and take a bit of time off each day. Step away and maybe toward a magical sea-green rocky hillside or onto a nature path.

Free

If you have been working too much, you may have forgotten how it feels to be free. Step outside your door. Start slowly. It may seem foreign at first as you bask in the bright light of the sun above you as it soothes your skin with warmth. When you are no longer squinting your eyes, you'll notice the blue area (sky by day, space and stars by night) and maybe some clouds you once used to easily stop and gaze upon as a child. That *alive* green stuff coming into view and those colorful patches and things swaying in the wind, are grass, flowers and leaves! Forgive my bluntness. This is how I used to feel when I worked for too long—like I didn't recognize it. So if you don't get out enough, remember to step out into nature and smell, see, touch, and feel it often, even if some days it is only for a few minutes; do it for the human "nature" in you.

Taking my own advice, I stopped for five minutes while writing this tip. I called to our young adult son and said, "Hey, join me for a moment or two, I want to show you something on the sidewalk." Leaving his office chair, which he does not always do as quickly, together we made our way out of techno-world and out the front door. As we walked toward a tree a small bird flew near my son's head. Then we both lay down on the sun-heated sidewalk, consciously aware of the Earth under us, our bodies supported, as we simply breathed in and out for five minutes on our backs looking up!

The More Who Unplug and Play in Nature Each Day the Merrier!

Use technology to shorten your workday and then turn it off and take a complete rest from it! Let your friends and family know where you are when you unplug and tell them when you are turning off your technology. Invite them to join you in enjoying breathing, walking, running, jumping, dancing, playing, singing and laughing.

If you have lost touch with nature and what it means to touch the Earth, reconnect by walking to a nearby stream, feeling the wind in your hair, or rolling down a grassy hill. Don't be surprised if you bump into others on that hill who have unplugged too. The more people who respectfully enjoy nature in love, laughter, and play the merrier.

Nature Walk to a Café

If you need to give yourself incentive to get away from overwork, book a self-care appointment with nature as you would with any other health appointment—except that nature doesn't charge. Don't think of taking these appointments with nature because something is wrong with

you; take it in the opposite attitude that something is *right* as you breathe fresh air and stroll. If you need incentive, plan to go to a café if it helps you demagnetize from your chair, inviting couch potatoes or office junkies whom you may desire to join you. Enjoy your re-energizing and refreshing walk ... sun overhead, wind in your hair, looking at the trees, clouds or stars in the sky, feeling the precious Earth beneath you, on your way to the café or your "appointment" with *nature*!

Blooming Lovely: Put a Bit of Nature in Your Office or Home Today

Depending where you live, whether there are leaves on the ground, seaweed or sand by the shore, or shells, or stones—even a twig will do—bring a few of these natural wonders into your home or office. Do you like flowers or green plants? Put a couple of flowers floating in a bowl of water nearby for you to enjoy. If you have access to foliage, put some on your table or desk so you can see, touch, smell and enjoy it. Remember to put these precious bits of nature back where you found them after you are finished enjoying them.

Stones: Healing Energy from Time Immemorial

Simply looking at, touching or sitting by large stones, or climbing on big rocks, is a way to enjoy nature's stillness. Rocks, gems, stones, and crystals can all be used to soothe your body. If you are like many people, you may keep a rock or crystal collection. If you have one, but you forgot about it, enjoy sitting near or holding your stones in silence when you want to be soothed.

If you haven't got any rocks or stones gather some next time you're outside. If you like you can buy an eco-friendly marker and write a *care* word or phrase like Rest, Care, or Gentle onto each stone. Leave these stones lying here, there, anywhere. This is an affordable and easy way to place nature and caring thoughts for you and others, anywhere. Eventually, the marker will wear off, or if you return the stones to the environment, their word journey ended, they will go back to *no words*, natural, and in their own element again.

Sunset, Starlight, Sunrise

My husband and I love to watch beautiful sunsets or the stars at night, sitting on our patio chairs together. If you have not sky-gazed lately, find an evening to stroll at sunset or to sit out on the porch and watch the stars. If you are not too tired, find the time to get up early one morning with a hot drink for a quiet time and watch the sunrise. There are 365 sunrises, sunsets and evening skies per year, so there is no excuse to miss them. Take time to enjoy the skies with those you care about—it is basic to our humanity.

Ocean Waves, Flowing Rivers, Clean Lakes, Drinking Streams

Water speaks in so many ways and our own body knows this flowing language on an inside level. We are developed in and birthed through water; in the beginning, it is our mini-ocean, our home. When we care for the waters of creeks, rivers, lakes, and the oceans, we give *ourselves* life for they *are* the waters we love to drink, cool, soothe and cleanse with, swim and play in.

Those who dwell
Among the ecologies, animals, and oceans of the Earth
Are never without a friend or disappointed with life.
—Marilyn Idle

Home Remedies for Sore Throat

It is not necessary to fear or pop in pills when you have a sore throat, especially if the symptoms are still mild. Rather, you can use some easy at home soothing care. In case you want to know how to quickly get rid of sore throat naturally, read on.

- The first line of defence is to gargle with warm, salt water every few hours.
- My grandpa used to grow, make and drink chamomile tea and now I understand why. It has pain-relieving properties that can provide you quick relief from throat pain and headaches.
- Oregano or sage, either in the form of tincture or in the form of capsules are herbs you can learn more about. They can reduce inflammation and support and protect the soft tissues of the throat as well as the respiratory system. Most people are now aware that adding fresh garlic or onion to foods can add anti-bacterial properties.
- Gargle every few hours with unsweetened cranberry or pomegranate juice which is diluted to your taste with water. It will help get rid of infective invaders. Avoid sugar until your throat feels better. The effects of sugar can make immune function sluggish for several hours and it's acidic so it can increase inflammation.
- An age old favorite drink to soothe you is warm tea with honey and it provides throat calming relief. For a different warm beverage which has an anti-bacterial "punch", add to your honey tea, one teaspoon of cinnamon and a pinch of ginger and sip slowly.

Turn Dis-Ease Season into Wellness Season!

I am infected with an infinite case of wellness and it's contagious. After twenty years of experience and research in the area of whole-person immunity and wellness I choose to heal my mind and body with non-synthetics ... namely, natural *food!* I have watched billions of dollars swallowed up by the unhealthy parts of a medical-pharmaceutical corporate world and while I respect and appreciate its many miraculous trauma care results, I reject its disease-drug-profit side. It is wrought with too many medical-dependency-causing and dismal results which do little to support or celebrate the whole person, I am. Instead, I chose a diet of mainly fresh, organic, naturally growing foods and spices, which if I want to, I can literally grow for myself. We are moving back to real food nutrition and toward a system of natural care with thoughtful doctors of integrity evolving bridges to preventative wellness balanced with medical or trauma care, only as needed. Good doctors who support common sense, prevention and drug-free wellness do not make as much money as disease-profiting doctors, therefore, when you find a good one make sure to invest in regular visits and tell your friends about them.

Don't Get Under the Weather: Ride on Top of It

Some people feel the Earth's weather changes in their nerves, muscles, and bones, and this can be quite distressing if you don't know what is happening. I know because I am a human weather barometer! If you too are sensitive and feel changes in the weather (or maybe you have super-hero sensing powers in experiencing shifts in Earth's energies) you are not going crazy! The ability to perceive the Earth's changes in your bones and body is not a sickness! It may be tempting to disbelieve, but a farmer who is in touch with nature and the seasons might grin, tilt their head back, and gently laugh at you!

It might be tempting to numb yourself with painkillers or drink more alcohol to help. Yet, it is better to embrace and love yourself while respecting your connection with the Earth and sky as they play their music on your bones. As you learn to ride with the Earth, its weather and seasonal changes, take it easy on yourself on those transition days. You may need to just be quiet and lie down for a few moments or longer several times a day during weather shifts. Even if you must be at work, take time every hour to smooth your "ruffled feathers" or to slowly breathe more deeply as needed until you acclimatize.

If you feel achy, tired, confused, or emotional take sixty seconds whenever you need it and comfort or rest. If you are at home take mini-power-naps or crawl onto your sofa or bed and curl up like a bear hibernating for as many minutes or hours as you can allow yourself. Now that you know you are not ill, but simply in touch with the throbbing of Earth, you need not be anxious, or annoyed. The Earth and skies are talking to you! (I can see my farming ancestors who were so close to the Earth smiling).

Cave, Forest, Lake, Creek

Explore something new in nature. If you live in a place where there are caves, a forest, river, or lake, take an hour, or a day if you can, to explore! Leave a trip-plan so someone could find you if necessary. Pack out what you pack in and leave no trace that you were there but your love.

Seaweed for Your Body's Inner Ocean

Eating seaweed harvested from the ocean, whether dried or in capsules, brings the ocean's natural minerals to you. The minerals and natural iodine in seaweed can help you be well in many ways, including supporting your thyroid function. Mineral rich emerald green seaweed can *shore up* your body. Harvest seaweed directly from the ocean, or get it at your local health food store. You may begin to see why the ocean's watery garden is so rich and enlivening to your health.

Nature's Nutritive Table Dispenser

Recently, I heard that pharmaceutical companies will soon be placing automated prescription drug dispensers, similar to drive-through cash machines, in remote communities where drugstores are sometimes not available. So, I decided to co-opt the idea for my home! I haven't had any need for prescription drugs for almost twenty years now, since I learned about natural wellness and took responsibility for my health. I am able to remain well or return to balance quickly using natural foods, herbs, walks, rest, relaxation, fun, and good thoughts. I thought, "I can put one of these dispensers on my table. But instead of drugs, I will put spices, seeds, nuts, dried berries, and fruit in it and dispense away—happily and without guilt!"

I found a spice rack with ten little jars. In each one I placed body-supportive foods. As I write this tip, there are dried sugarless cranberries, raw sunflower seeds, pumpkin seeds, dried coconut, kelp, sesame seeds, nutritional yeast, candied ginger, raw cashew nuts, raw almonds, dried bananas, and Gobi berries. These foods have body building enzymes, protein, essential vitamins, good fats, fatty acids, and minerals such as calcium, magnesium, potassium and iodine.

The nutrition dispenser is nature's wellness support, easy to understand, affordable and right within reach in full view. It reminds me and my family to eat a little of this or that as needed. What will you put on *your* table?

Thunderstorms

Some people find thunderstorms scary. I love them. If you are having a thunderstorm in your area, without putting yourself at any risk, and only if the storm is still off in the distance, sit out on your patio or cuddle up on the living room sofa near a window and just listen to the thunder and watch the lightning.

Vibrations Affect You

Your finely balanced living systems and processes (bio-electric) are affected by vibrations: Music and words can be healing, stirring, supportive, soothing, calming, or disturbing, and can even cause harm. Sound at more than 120 decibels can damage the eardrums in a very short time and shockwaves from large explosions can easily damage the body.

Many competing sounds for long periods of time is now defined as noise pollution in North America, Europe, and other urbanized parts of the world. This assault harms people and wildlife. We are turning this around. More people today understand the need for conscious mutual respect of our shared *hearing space*, and the dangers of harmful ubiquitous sound. Be thoughtful of the sounds and vibrations you make in your environment, being sure you do not disturb or hurt other people or living creatures. Sometimes the most healing sound of all is silence.

Water Brings Balance!

So simple is this self-care with water tip, that you could overlook it. Don't! I cannot stress enough the importance of water in wellness. Water is the universal solvent and it can flush and support your body and help you to rebalance quicker than any drug, food, or herb. With water to support you, your body can eliminate headaches or anxiety attacks, dilute acid burning in your stomach, eliminate toxins like alcohol, dissolve food reactions, end hormone flashes, and support your eliminatory and immune systems.

When you or someone you love is feeling under the weather, it can be tempting to look for complicated, expensive medications or treatments. But, consider drinking pure water while you decide what you will do, because caring for the seventy percent water part of you can help. Water, the world's greatest purifier and cleanser, even soothes inflamed muscles after stressful exertion. When I type too much, my fingers, hands, arms, shoulders, neck and jaw can become over-tired and begin to feel on fire. Now, I keep a glass of water and a wet cloth next to me; I sip and soothe regularly, giving my hands and face a mini-bath with a cool cloth or splash of water!

Imagine when you drink water that you've dipped your glass into an absolutely pure creek, like those we once had on Earth. When you get outside, and hopefully that is soon, find a creek or river and put your hands or toes in it to connect with nature's splashing, soothing ways.

How Much Water Do You Need for Your Unique Body?

Some experts say that to calculate an appropriate water intake for your body and size, you should take half of your body weight in pounds and then multiply that amount by one ounce of water. However, your need for water is unique to you, the food you eat and your lifestyle. Observing whether the foods you eat are water rich or not, and listening to your body, *you* decide the amount of water you will drink. One way to help you to listen to your body's water wisdom is to keep a glass of pure water near you. Having it in front of you will alert your busy mind to take a break and your hand to reach for as much water as you need!

Spending Time with Animals

Animals live in balance and harmony with the waters, minerals, soils, cycles, and seasons of the Earth. Spending time with animals or watching them is healing. It teaches you to enjoy your life in awareness of other living beings.

Watching nature shows with your children is a perfect time to teach how technology can have good uses, like respectfully filming lions, beluga whales, polar bears, or penguins in ways most of us have never seen before. Yet, technology can also be used to bombard and even bomb dolphins, sharks, blue whales, and people. With the new kinds of close-up footage filmed by respectful humans, your kids can be amazed and learn new understandings about our world in a way that always seeks to care.

Have You Heard About Ear-Soothing Wildflowers?

Organic herbal ear oil wonderfully calms an earache and is available from most health stores. You can protect and soothe your family's ears with nature's calm, often in less than fifteen minutes. If you have nothing else on hand a drop of cold pressed organic olive oil gives soothing and relieving ear care. If you are swimming in waters that are of questionable purity, or if you go to a highly chlorinated public pool, keep this blend on hand especially if you have young children or work with them. If you find it as helpful as our family did, you may have to keep it always on hand in the refrigerator.

Nature's ear support and care blend: Always use organic cold pressed oils. Olive is protective; calendula soothes the skin; woolly mullein soothes tissues and is decongestive; St. John's wort is calming (nature's Prozac); lavender is antibiotic; and garlic is blood cleansing.

One of Nature's Amazing Herbs: Oil of Oregano

Our family has a very contagious case of wellness most of the time now. However, a number of winters ago, I arrived at my mom's sunny home after a long succession of airplane flights. I was taken aback when cold or viral symptoms started coming on strong. Three older women friends were visiting as well and they quietly and knowingly looked at me. I thought, "I bet they aren't glad I'm here!" But they smiled and said in unison, "Try oregano oil drops." "No," I said, "it's too late, look at me. I'll just have to stay in bed and heal for as long as it takes."

Given how terrible I felt this seemed like the only option, although I've always been told once it's here a cold or flu "runs its course." My mom said, "Why don't you try it? You have nothing to lose!" So, I put a drop under my tongue every three hours that night, knowing it was useless, but *what the heaven*, I was in no shape to argue. By morning, every single symptom was gone. Now you understand why this new addition to our medicine cabinet also goes anywhere we travel!

Some months later, after several long days downhill skiing in the cold, my partner developed similar symptoms and a smile formed on my face. I went out and got more of the powerful little *nature-in-a-bottle* oregano drops. It has been almost ten years since we learned the value of this useful little herb, which surpasses everything in our medicine cabinet in supporting each of us. It is a balancing food that works in harmony with your body's chemistry and ecology. In ancient Babylonia and Greece, oregano or "delight of the mountains" was known as one of nature's most potent healing plants.

It is non-toxic; it abates bacteria, viruses, yeast, fungi, and mold; reverses inflammation; supports elimination; and makes you less hospitable to super-bug bacterial invaders. Do some more research on your own, and if you want to, try it. For children, I add honey and lemon and give it to them on a spoon in spicy, sweet liquid drops.

Bitters: Sweet Helpers in Removing Heavy Metals

Your body's own cleansing mechanism daily naturally removes heavy metals from your cells, which may be in your body from environmental pollutants like car exhaust, chemical herbicides and pesticide residues on food, cans, mercury dental fillings, hair dye, and so on. Every cell of your body makes natural *chelating* agents that combine with these toxins and carry them out of the body, yet as we age, our cells often function less well in this way depending on what foods we eat. So, over our lifetime it is good practice to add more chelating foods to your diet.

There are an abundance of homemade foods you can eat that offer healthy body support through natural chelation. Coriander, also called cilantro, is one of the herbs that can help your body to remove heavy metals. Organic raw apple cider vinegar, fermented foods, natural plants sugars, and even cold pressed fats like organic olive oil can act as effective chelators. Lentils, lima beans, potatoes, garlic, onions, and herbs such as Italian parsley, yellow dock root, hibiscus, sheep sorrel, and other plants high in vitamin C have a natural ability to help your body remove heavy metals too.

Some of the most effective chelating agents can be found in the soil we walk on and the water we drink. Bentonite clay mixed with pure water works amazingly well as a purifier, but their quality is critical in detoxification from heavy metals.

Though I didn't understand the significance until later in my life, I now recollect my grandparents (the ones who made it through wars and plagues and lived well into their nineties) ate most of the items I have listed here as part of their regular diets. They probably never knew this was helping them to live long and well. Your ancestors have been utilizing nature's own heavy metal removal and body wellness support for thousands of years, so now, how about you and your children?

Using Infinity to See Better!

This tip is about using your inner nature, mind's eye, or imagination, as well as a "nose paintbrush" to draw an infinity sign intended to connect and activate your right and left brain vision centers. Imagine that your nose is like Pinocchio's and grow it into an energy paintbrush. Use the paintbrush to paint white light or color around the object or words you want to see more clearly. Try this whenever your eyes feel tired or your sight is blurry. Just stop what you're doing and nose-brush-paint an infinity sign. Infinity is represented in math by a symbol that looks like a sideways eight. You can make it small or large and on anything, such as a wall or a book page.

By calming yourself, taking a few moments, and allowing the exercises to flow naturally, you can learn *how* to see. (For more on natural eye care, see *The Practical Guide to Natural Vision Improvement* by Carina Goodrich, from which I adapted this exercise.)

Tension Affects Vision

After hours on the computer or reading books, I'd strain my eyes to see. I learned about natural vision and now understand the many levels of 'seeing' and how to take care of my eyes. I learned from Carina Goodrich that our eyes don't need further force or strain, they need to relax, to rest, to learn to see in our unique work or life circumstances and they like to play!

Eye-Care from the Sun

This nature tip, using the sun to support natural vision, may not be popular for those who sell glasses! I found a book about natural vision care, and wow, my eyes were opened! Yet for this sunning of your eyes, they must be closed!

Our eyesight has developed over the eons in partnership with the sun. We humans are evolutionarily known as diurnal (day) creatures. Keeping your eyes closed let the sun's light infuse your face. Breathe deeply and imagine the sun's fiery rays as the petals of a sunflower. Moving your eyes behind their closed lids, gently draw a clockwise circle around the sun's rays or *petals* with your eyes. (Imagine your nose has an extendable pencil or paintbrush on the end of it, to help you touch the sun and imagine drawing the circles around the sun's rays.) Continuing to breathe deeply use your mind's eye to draw a stem to the Sunflower down into the Earth with imaginary roots. Allow yourself to be filled, as if by liquid, using the sun's bright light. Doing this can strengthen your vision in ten to sixty seconds daily, even on cloudy days.

Stages of Life on Earth

For me, living in nature usually feels very beautiful, but at times it seems quite the opposite. When I look at life from the perspective of infinite love, with no judgement at all, I realize that my body is just one part of who I am. When I take my last breath and shed my body it will become part of the planet again, a canvas for new life. To some that may not seem beautiful, and in the past it was not for me. I now understand better how life works on Earth. I am humbled and grateful even for the "not so beautiful" stages, like how soil comes from the end of life, the shedding of form after physical death.

The cycles of life do not have to be scary or sad. For me there is no death, only *change* from one infinite life form to another. That is why I have come to love everything: because I feel that from the smallest rock, mineral or cell to the largest tree, animal, elephant, or blue whale (the largest creature on the planet currently), from a larger infinite view, we are separate, yes, yet all part of a whole—*one*.

Everyone and everything comes from and returns to infinite love. That, to me, is the meaning of the word *sacred*. Nothing and no one gets lost or left behind, just changed. Living on Earth is one beautiful, yet sometimes scary and hard, finite *bodily* life within infinity.

50

Balance, Vitality and Life Energy

This is a chapter about creating balance in your life and the de-stressing and relief that brings.

One step I've used to balance my life has been to live as simply as possible. This has involved figuring out what really matters to me. For example, kindness, family and friends, living in harmony with nature, and having fun. Simplifying and focusing on what I care about most has always helped me. Balance is vital to happiness because it's a form of harmony. It helps you to be well and happy.

I used to have a life that was so busy, overloaded, filled with activity, meetings, and long fast-paced workdays that my stomach began to feel the way it did the first time I walked the balance beam in gym class. That beam looked easy, yet when I got up in the air, going faster and faster, it became harder to stay on top of it! Trying to make it to the end of the beam quickly, I'd begin wobbling, flapping, and flailing my arms, and every time, if I didn't slow down and rebalance, I'd fall off. Similarly, I needed to stop and re-balance my life.

It takes time and effort to learn what works for you, especially if your work, family, or others have demands of you that don't suit your personal nature or daily rhythms. Living a simpler life does not promise that all will be well, yet it gives you more time for rest, relaxation, play and fun. If you feel overloaded with internal and external pressures and you want more relaxation, peace, wellness, and balance, this can at first seem very difficult to do. Who and what do you say *no* to? How can you take time for yourself when so many others demand that you don't stop?

Learning how to re-balance and simplify my life, I went through many hours of frustration, tears, tension, thought, consideration, deliberations, reflections, observation, and I had to take some time to just rest and heal. As I learned new ways of self-care, some of which I have shared in this book, I eventually found *my* ways!

Finding *your* way to balance may not happen overnight, yet this is why I put sixty-second tips in this book! That is how I started since I could only afford to give myself sixty seconds to breathe. Though life on Earth is short, I now realize I have infinity to breathe; or maybe I'm breathing infinity now even while I'm here for a short while. Either way, I take time now when I need it and I invite you to as well.

I now love living a downsized life and I am always looking for ways to simplify more. Less is better at home, at business, at work. Owning fewer things means less to keep-watch-out-for-and-take-care-of. Smaller home size equals less house cleaning and fewer dust bunnies. The way you can tell you have too many things in your family is if your life feels full yet empty of the peace, self, relationship time, and nature-loving moments that matter the most.

Balance Power with Gentleness

I used to be very demanding of myself and would power-work some days into the wee hours, and then be so tired and empty I'd just drop. Or, I'd become "sick" or hurt so much I couldn't even enjoy being peaceful or playful when I finally took precious time off. Today I believe there is no such thing as sickness, there is only lack of balance and a body's various ways of showing that! It is one thing to occasionally work to finish a project on a timeline, but there are ways to do it with peace and gentle care.

If you think that overwork, too many things, credit card debt, or any form of unhealthy lifestyle has been too long in overdrive for you and your family, and if you have concern and compassion about how hard this can be on your body, personal life, and family, stop and balance now. Gently

find your own way to downsize: work hard, yet also to be free and playful, in perfect balance. You can be.

As Much as Possible Free Yourself of Things

Having too much stuff can unconsciously make you feel weighed down, worrying about and guarding everything. Here is a simple and loving way to create balance: If your home feels over-stuffed, sell or give away the things that you don't use, even if you think you might need them some year! If you need it in future, go out and get it then! After you lighten up avoid packing in more bits and pieces. When you go shopping, ask yourself, "Do I *really* need this?" Sometimes, if I overfill my shopping cart (usually if I'm hungry), just before heading to the cashier I think, "Can I do without this?" Most often I happily put back needless items. My family and I are able to share happiness and abundance in other ways and don't miss the things I didn't buy: I can't even remember what they were!

52

Time with Friends and Family

Your family and friends are the ones who see you at your worst and best. These are the people who will catch you when you fall, so be kind to them and be there for them too. (Some families are not healthy, so this tip also refers to people you choose as family.) No matter how busy you get or how important your message, mission, work, or pursuits become to you, always take time to be with the people who love you. After all is said and done, being and exchanging love is what all the work and business of life and living are really about, isn't it?

Who will you ask to spend some time with you soon?

Embracing Yourself Helps You Rest, Relax, and Unwind

Do you sometimes feel so wound up (perhaps from forgetting to take regular re-balance and unwind stops) that when it's finally time to turn off, relax, or sleep, your head, body and muscles stay *on*? If you feel on high speed even when it is time for you to rest or sleep don't fight yourself. You may be exhausted, yet wide-awake, due to tension, aches, artificial light or technologies. Gently accept yourself in this state. Cozy up in bed, play some music to touch your heart and soothe you. Or, if you are too agitated to get in bed, curl up in a soft, fluffy comforter in a chair and sip a hot cup of tea. Literally hug yourself. Embrace and care for you, just the way you are. By allowing yourself to be as you are instead of putting more energy into feeling upset, your nerves, body, and consciousness can shift to a lower speed, not by more force, but by feeling your own kind heart while holding yourself in warmth and doing absolutely nothing. Let the waves of calm wash over you when they do and simply be there, breathing, quiet, comforting, caring for you; with no force, only relief and compassion.

No More Multi-tasking! One Thing at a Time

I laugh when I think of this tip because I am a high-speed multi-tasker from way back. However, it brings me peace to do one thing at a time. When I get out of balance from trying to do too many things at once, I slow down and focus almost meditatively on one. My once roaring pace transforms to a purr.

By putting your full focus on one activity at a time you can do your best work. My happiest most loving accomplishments, for me or for others, are done one step at a time, thoughtfully, lovingly, and meditatively. Put love before quantity. Doing fewer things at the same time allows you to breathe and to do that.

Balancing Criticism with Appreciation

I love it when someone compliments, appreciates, or thanks me. Receiving constructive criticism is harder. I find I can utilize criticism most easily when it gets to the point but is also offered with a healthy helping of loving support.

When talking with your partner, child, or co-worker add a caring and respectful comment to any constructive criticism you may want to deliver. For example, you could say something like this to your child: "To me, you are overall a very loving and thoughtful person who cares well for your home and things. Today, you threw your wet towel on the floor and I had to pick it up before I could step into the shower. Please hang your towels on the towel rack. Thank you very much." Whether or not the receiver can, in that moment, hear only criticism from you, nonetheless, you have offered your input in a caring and balanced way. You have also given a love-filled and kind thank you.

Transform Insults into Self-Love

Try this when you're frustrated. If you tend to say statements to yourself like "You're an idiot" (jerk, dumb, loser), immediately balance that with, "I am smart" (a fair person, a winner). It neutralizes and frees you. Words and sounds are vibration. Thought balancing is fun. You can decide if your words vibrate usefully or not. It is incredibly empowering to take an insulting or put-down phrase whether from you or others and change it to a positive expression with new meaning. You get the idea.

Road to Wellness Detox with Daily Mini-Cleanses

With the increasing overload of pollutants over the last fifty years, our bodies' detoxifying organs have become stressed to the max. This has to turn around now. We are being exposed to approximately 90,000 *new* chemicals and hundreds of new super bacterial, fungal, and viral strains each year. Much of our food, by the way it is produced, has increasingly and wrongly become a source of toxins from the array of *whatever-icides* or gene-altered foods we are now consuming. Most of these were non-existent twenty years ago.

I admit I love the instant gratification of eating chemically enhanced lip smacking foods and drinks, but their food value and life force is nil. Beyond that, omigosh, many of these foods are proving to be actual poison to us, and by association, to our nature, land, sea, air and wildlife.

I'm not saying we have to be the boy or girl in the bubble and never eat processed or questionable food, yet we can do better than that. We are waking up, but many people still are unknowingly poisoning themselves. When teens visit my son and bring chips, candy, pop, and so on, for snacks, I tell them it would be great to do a mini-cleanse right afterwards. I explain to them, while offering whatever-icide-free fresh fruit, veggies, seeds, nuts, or lemon water, that eating some of these will help the liver get rid of *pesti-chemi-poisons* in the dead food.

These powerful natural foods can wash away the toxic, addictive effects of chemically "enhanced" foods such as, saturated body clogging or overheated fats, preservatives, pesticides, chemicals, colors, artificial sweeteners, salt, sugar. I suggest eating healthier food right away, food that is more respectful of body and Earth. Sometimes I'll offer the kids organic junk foods, which are not much more nutritious than processed snack foods, yet at least deliver no chemical or genetically modified toxins.

You might wonder why I don't just shake my finger and recommend not eating processed foods at all. The reason is that I eat them sometimes, millions of people love them, and we are in this together. So we must share ways to make junk food healthier! If you eat or drink these tasty commercial-chemical foods, also have a piece of celery or a refreshing sip of pure water with lemon or lime afterwards. Before or after you eat yummy dead chemical chips, also eat one teaspoon of raw sunflower, or pumpkin seeds, or a couple of almonds. These contain essential fats your liver can use to do its detoxification job.

Top off luscious harmful fatty french fries made from chemically treated potatoes and possibly unhealthy GMO soy or corn oils, with a generous helping of cleansing foods. Before or after eating greasy or denatured things, eat some fresh organic vegetables like carrot, celery or cucumber or liver-supporting herbs such as parsley or cilantro. These help you break down and eliminate fat and can help to draw heavy metals from pesticides used on conventional produce and remove environmental pollution out of your body.

Balance every day with these healthy chasers and body supportive mini-cleanses every time you eat enjoyable but valueless "fun food."

Balance Coffee Break

If you only have a fifteen minute break at work, it may feel easier to remain indoors and have another quick cup of coffee; or, if you work at home, to sit in front of the TV or computer. Yet you may feel like you would enjoy getting out for some fresh air but there isn't enough time.

Here is an answer. Go outside for a two-minute mini fresh-air walk! One minute out and one minute back, and you will refresh yourself and have moved your body, having touched the Earth and taken a big deep breath under the sky. Some days your mini-walk may be four minutes, or some days if the weather is wonderful your walk may be ten minutes or more. Just remember two minutes outside daily or whenever you desire it, is better than zero minutes!

Running Late? Stop and Balance

When running late for a meeting or completing a goal don't stress out. Instead stop and breathe for just ten to sixty seconds. You could continue to rush and stress out or say things to yourself like "I'm late, oh no," while heightening your worries about what being late may cause. Or, you can stop, breathe, and ask, "How can I make things work out in the best most balanced way for all concerned, even now?"

When you shift your thoughts to balancing and calming ones, you have used the power of your stress-energy to actually help you and not further hinder you. Then when you arrive, even if a bit late, you are in a relaxed condition with lots of energy to benefit you and everyone. You may prefer you were not late, yet you are, and now whatever happens when you arrive, you have used your energy wisely to fuel a powerful result.

Set Aside One Night Each Week for Play

Turn off the cell phone, shut down the computer, and unplug your TV. Choose one night to take completely off for play each week. If the idea of shutting things down and playing in peace and with no technology seems bizarre or impossible, you know it's the right thing to do! Play on your own, play with your dog or kitty (they're always ready to play), be in the good company of your partner, someone in your family, nature, or a friend. Give people the heads-up and invite them a few days earlier so everyone can unplug at the same time. Get some ideas together that you might want to enjoy: games, dancing around, singing, walking, canoeing, or creating a new out of the ordinary adventure.

Balance from Communicating Clearly

Sometimes when we most need to play or rest, we squander these precious moments by tiredly rehashing argumentative scenarios with others. This is likely because you or they are in pain, tired, or are only half-listening, which easily leads to misunderstanding. Why not stop for a few moments of calm and rebalance? This is not a 911 emergency, so don't waste any time shouting muddled communications that are destined to fail. Instead, look in the other person's eyes and tell them you want to calm and rest first. Later, you can both begin sharing, understanding, and responding using what will be much more carefully chosen and helpful words.

Are You Getting Enough Sleep?

There's nothing more stressful or destructive of balance than being sleep-deprived. It steals your day from you like nothing else. Not only is your thinking and efficiency affected, but also, you tend to make judgments that hurt you or others. It may take days to make it up to those you have hurt or to fix your mistakes that were caused mainly from exhaustion. A few late nights happen for all of us, but find a way to get enough sleep!

Earn a Living Doing What You Love and Spend Less Money Than You Make!

As much as you can, unite what fascinates or impassions you with how you earn a living. A good portion of your life will be spent working so if there is little meaning or enthusiasm in your daily work it could have a depressing, unbalancing effect on you. Following your passion may earn you more or less money, but money will not be your prime motivator.

Many people have found they are happiest doing what they love, living debt-free and simply. This can be hard to do if you live in an expensive city where at every corner a billboard ad from a bank or credit card company says debt is normal. It may be normal to live beyond your means yet it is not a balanced way to live and it certainly is not natural. Whatever work you choose to do and wherever in the world you choose to live, do not buy in to credit. Spend less than you make. I believe debt is the biggest imbalance of this century. If *you* are in debt, find a healthy way to get out as quickly as you can—then stay out of debt!

Leaping While Taking One Step at a Time

Everyone, at some point, will face a loss, a life-jolting problem, a goal stopping challenge, or a mess to figure out. With each step you must take remember to face this challenge with love, daily self-care, and balance. If you can leap out or over your challenge immediately, then do it! If not, then while you are sorting things out take one balanced self-caring step at a time. Celebrate each step, and don't ever give up!

Don't Let Work Spill into Your Personal Life

With a global economy, new international business connections, and all the new communication technologies, many of us find longer work hours creeping into our lives. Some people are *never* away from work! Dual-career couples face particular challenges when their children and parenting roles must be handed over to relatives or daycares. Many feel pressured to work harder, longer, and produce more just to protect their jobs. Because we can now work from anywhere this continues around the world twenty-four hours a day from home, our cars, and even while on vacation! This overwork makes it difficult to find simple balance or time to meet commitments to love, cherish, and enjoy family, children, friends, the Earth, and its life and community.

There was a time when you showed up for work Monday through Friday. You left your home in the morning and returned at suppertime and complained about having to work on holidays after an eight to twelve hour day! Now, the world has changed. For a very few this old separation between work and personal life still exists, but for many the separation between work and home is no longer clear or not there at all!

Because work and personal time have blurred for so many of us, understanding what is going on is important so that you can recreate your life in a way that nourishes you and your family. If you don't stop and create a lifestyle with boundaries and balance, you, your relationships, and your home life will likely pay the price.

Learning from Others

It's fun to share stories and knowledge; we help each other when we communicate what we have been through and learned. Others' lifestyles, goals and dreams may be quite different from yours, yet we are all similar when it comes to wanting happiness, adventure, balance, wellness, and peace. Observe others who are happy, peaceful, or seem to live a *quality* life. What are they doing that you may want to try? Do they have a way of thinking that frees them to do what really matters? Talk with them and learn from them.

Co-respectful, Sustainable Living for 7,000,000,000

This is a chapter about living happily, self-responsibly and co-respectfully with others and earth.

Give me one good reason
seven billion of us, universal friends on the planet, couldn't help each other
make our ecology, people, and animal-respecting goals true, now
—there isn't one.
—Marilyn Idle

There are now nearly seven billion people on Earth and we must take care of this beautiful planet through careful and thoughtful protection of our soils, airways, and waterways. In turn the Earth will care for us. The toxic economy is polluting our precious Earth and all its inhabitants. It is time to change direction for our current ways will not sustain life.

The economy, as we have set it up in the last one hundred years, is falling down. Corporations who think only of selling more *things* are failing. Most everyone now realizes that to take more than nature can replenish is an invitation for premature human demise.

If the things you and I buy are made in ways that harm many but profit few, strip nature, indebt or starve people, destroy ecosystems, treat animals appallingly, and misguide our children, then surely we must stop. The good news is that we *are* changing toward leave-no-trace-ecology-respecting ways. An innovative, sustainable, ecology-balanced era is here now. We are learning to combine technology with nature-respecting paths.

It is not through fighting that this change is happening, but by bringing new co-respecting ways to live—like powerful, simple cooperation, everyone doing their job, large or small. Many young people are developing new ways to live and adventure with zero debt, zero waste, zero emissions, and sustainable safer energy!

If you are one of the inspired ones, wise, whole, and awake, thank you. If you are not, I know you may soon be. Then, with your deepest gifts emerging, perhaps you too will help make your backyard, this Earth, a seventh heaven. My husband asked, "Where are the other six?" My answer ... "Are we—on Earth, really the first to achieve this balanced, heavenly state of living?"

Taste your tears.
You are the ocean.
—Marilyn Idle

Oceans Coming Back: Dead Zones to Living Zone

I have been to the ocean only twice, my son only once, when he was very young. We both fell in love with the sea. I watched him run in yellow rubber boots in the sand foam, and taught him how to walk with thoughtful care at low tide to see the life.

At the time I did not know that the oceans make fifty percent of the Earth's oxygen. I see the ocean as a vast colorful dream come true: smelling the salt air, touching the water, seeing the multitudes of harmonious life and vegetation.

Our son was four at the time and was fascinated by the creatures: the orange and purple starfish, the little blue and red crabs, purple and orange sea anemones revealed attached to rocks at low tide. Then at night, bluish flickers visible in the water and sparkling in the wet sand, these were blooms of ocean dinoflagellates.

Recently, I learned that the National Aeronautics and Space Administration (NASA) has taken photos from space which reveal that our oceans have many *dead zones* which do not create oxygen anymore. That means the coastal life I just described, which spoke in living visual poetry to me, is dying. In the last one hundred years large corporations and farms have allowed chemicals, herbicides and pesticides to "run off" into the environment. It is difficult, if not impossible, for nature to break down these chemicals. They work their way into our oceans creating dead-zone sludge rather than oxygenated and oxygenating life.

Ecology-friendly business and farming methods can help reverse this, rebalancing our soils and waterways, thus supporting the coastal ocean ecology again. We need to reverse the effects of our past and current overuse of chemicals and farm fertilizers, which do end-flow harm after reaching the ocean shore. Unnatural fertilizer nutrients cause phytoplankton to overgrow, which leads to more organic matter reaching the ocean bottom, causing more bacterial activity and a more anoxic (lacking oxygen) environment in the ocean water. Industry chemicals, slowly or immediately, kill—life.

These dead zones, which are occurring in many areas along the coasts of major continents, are spreading over larger areas of the sea floor. Because few organisms can tolerate heavy metals, synthetic industry toxins or the lack of oxygen, this destroys the environment where they (used to) make their homes, causing them to move, adapt or die off. It's much easier for you and me to stop contributing to this, to bring our coasts back to life as oxygen producing zones, than it is for the ocean life to adapt.

Here is how: Buy eco-friendly products and food that is grown locally in well-cared-for soil and water. The food you eat doesn't have to be organic, just grown in sustainable, stewarded ways. As much as you can, stop buying gene modified seeds and foods. Until long-term safety is known, GMO have been hypothesized to be catalysts for increased antibody immune responses, opening the door to numerous health concerns. GMOs are "genetically modified organisms." Many farmers and scientists have blown the whistle on the corporations who produce them. They say they are one of the greatest threats *ever* to humans, animals, plants, seeds, and all of life.

59

Scores of ecology-enlightened businesses and food farmers are now moving away from harming or chemical methods and back to small nature and water-sustaining (or organic) ways, thus eliminating toxic residues. Support the people who are returning to ecology-friendly, leave-no-trace ways of living.

Sharks Protect Fifty Percent of the World's Ocean-Made Oxygen Supply!

Sharks play an important role in balancing oceanic ecologies. They are important contributors to the oceans' ongoing ability to make fifty percent of the Earth's oxygen supply. In the process of photosynthesis the oceans' phytoplankton releases oxygen into the water and herbivorous marine creatures eat the phytoplankton. Sharks which are carnivores, in turn, eat the herbivores preventing over-consumption of the oxygen producing plants. As human populations grow, this top-of-the-ocean-food-chain animal is killed en masse at alarming rates daily, to be made into shark fin soup. This is done without limit and without regard for the suffering of the sharks or the delicate oceanic cycles of life. If our oceans are imbalanced and sharks are unable to play their important role, fifty percent of Earth's oxygenation comes to a halt.

Did you know you are safer near a shark than you are on a highway, alongside another human? Shark populations need thoughtful understanding, care, and protection. How can you help care for sharks and the ocean? A good start is to understand the important role sharks play in the ocean-world plus realizing that in the larger picture of life on Earth caring for you and your body includes caring for oceanic life. With all of us participating in a caring way we will avoid unnecessary extinctions in our oceanic world while also protecting the planet's oxygen supplies.

Natural Seeds and Soil: Defenders of Humanity

In my view, no one owns nature or the Earth. We are stewards of it. According to an article by Carolyn Herriot, author of *A Year On The Garden Path: 52 Weeks Of Organic Gardening Guide and Zero Mile Diet*, in the last few years ninety-eight percent of the world's seeds are owned, and in many cases have been altered, patented, and sold by six corporations. This amazing fact is harmfully altering farmers' long held role of working with nature in their regions to grow foods in harmony with local soils, insects, organisms, animal biodiversity and weather conditions.

As Jim Scott posted on saltspringnews.com: "The people must lead: It's time to get REAL (regional and environmentally responsible agricultural land use)." Further, Jim says, "Current large farming methods rely on a system of agriculture dependent upon the use of herbicides, pesticides, petrochemicals and intensive irrigation. This system is non-renewable, non-sustainable, and generally non-local."

Biodiversity *is* life. Normally, if one seed, plant, or pollinating insect on a farm is hit by disease or poor weather, there are others that the farmer notices are naturally resistant. The farmer's observations and stewardship of many diverse species provide tried and true wisdom that can be applied to creating abundant and healthy crops. Every living organism has a role to play in our environment. If the Earth's farms and ecosystems are to return to health, we need to respect and protect the role of the farmer in each unique eco-sustainable farm.

Many families are now interested in learning where their food comes from and are having fun with their children growing food in patio pots, back yard gardens, and shared community plots. This is a good way to bring life back to Earth's soil. Earth's farming soils are so depleted and degraded that we may only have another fifty years of food production by way of chemicalized mega-farm soils, according to author and organic gardener, Carolyn Herriot.

Danna and her husband Brandon of O'Donnell's Garden Market and Organic Farm grow everything under the sun on their farm near my home. After arriving at Danna's organic market one tiring errand day, having shopped in stores full of colorful plastics, canned, cellophane-packed, imported, and pesticided produce, I was in tears. The relief and calm I felt, now away from the wound up complexity I had just left, brought such calm, simple sweet heaven that my body immediately responded with tears of healing joy.

I could smell the fresh natural peaches, plums, beets, carrots, many different squash, peppers of every color, potatoes, corn, pumpkins, grapes, yellow and red tomatoes, cucumbers and so much more—all grown in leave-no-trace, humane and no-harm-to-nature ways.

Healing tears continued to roll down my face as Danna quietly smiled. She told me that when she was a child her grandmother had no lawn in her backyard at all—she had all garden! Danna fondly remembered that as she would run freely through her grandma's garden her head would get hit by the shortest flowers, which were as tall as she was.

When I left the farm that day I was nourished deeply just by having been there for a few minutes. As I left, with a reusable cloth bag heaped with ripe pesticide-free vegetables, greens, and fruits, I looked back and saw a man in their lush green and color-filled huge garden. I waved and called, "Thank you and goodbye." Then, with a second look, noticing no returned goodbye wave, I saw that this hardworking man was actually the O'Donnell's Organic Market scarecrow, keeping vigil over the beautiful sustainable garden!

Join with other people in your community to grow local fruits and vegetables in planters, plots, backyard gardens, and fields. Learn from those who have taken good care of their egg-laying chickens, and allowed their animals to live freely in the fresh outdoors in the farms which are nearest to your community. As you learn, you will discover what life respecting, food growing or humane animal stewarding gifts you may secretly hold inside of you.

Bridging Medical and Dental Options with Wellness Approaches

Let me start by saying I love doctors and healthcare providers. I used to think of being a nurse when I was a little girl. I imagined how I'd save the wounded soldiers. Yet as I grew, I began to see that the for-profit medical system and the disaster-for-profit wars are both part of why soldiers are hurt. I would like to see us evolve to more understanding and friendship as peacemakers and wellness supporters, not out of control profiteers. There is little money to be made in friendship and wellness, yet both are good ways to avoid annihilating the human race.

I respect and work only with medical health care providers who understand and bridge with preventative and natural wellness. Every day, I learn more about what I need to do to prevent unnecessary, expensive medical and pharmaceutical interventions, and ways to use affordable, daily self-care and preventative wellness. Here is why: Most doctors, whom I visited from birth until I was a young woman, were not bridged with *any* options for self-empowered or preventative wellness, and they made me feel weaker, less confident about my body, and in some cases, unwell from their use of drugs. Using refined, patented, expensive pharmaceutical drugs and vaccines was not the path to wellness for me.

Taking herbs, flowers, leaves, sea vegetation, and water, with rest, work, and play in balance, was. And it made affordable sense. Drugs are best suited in the areas of trauma and emergency care when they are judiciously used. There are immune boosting alternatives to vaccines. Self-care is affordable to all and can be intelligently bridged to the best of what the medical field has to offer, predominantly in trauma care. Thoughtfully bridged with wellness, intelligent help from dedicated medical teams in place with equipment, pharmaceuticals, and highly skilled trauma-care support, makes good sense to me. Synthetic drugs, a vaccine for every possible invader, *and there are 1000's,* self unawareness and medical or dental dependency from birth on, doesn't.

Maybe you use only a "wait 'til it's sick or decayed then expensively drug, remove or replace-it" medical or dental approach, instead an affordable "maintain, rebuild 'n heal what you have" way to your overall health and if that works for you, all right! I believe many doctors, dentists and pharmacists have now become part of an expensive out-of-control profit-driven nightmare, which creates dependencies and does little or nothing to support wellness, self-knowledge, self-healing, and fear-free empowerment. Under extreme conditions of stress and abuse, my grandparents warded off or eliminated thousands of potential childhood, plague, and wartime dis-ease states naturally. How did they do that? Most often they did it simply and powerfully with sunshine, fresh air, lots of

sleep, good nutrition, fresh water, and living and working in harmony with nature. I do this now and so can you! (For free natural health ideas from a doctor, see www.mercola.com.)

Catch a contagious lasting case of wellness. Turn away from disease models and back toward the important question: "What do I truly need to be well today?" Just taking a little time daily for yourself in caring ways can keep you and your body flowing and well, in spite of the disease model and media fear stories. Simple daily care brings freedom, empowerment, a strong human spirit, healthy immune function and wellness to your life.

Heal Gums and Whiten and Maintain Tooth Enamel Naturally!

Smile After you brush your teeth, make a 50%-50% baking soda and Himalayan (or Sea) salt paste with a drop or two of 3% peroxide. (Use aloe if you have metal in your mouth.) Apply between teeth with a dental flosser and massage remaining paste at gum line with a soft baby toothbrush. Rinse with water. Your body knows how do the job of mending gum cells, jaw bone and tooth enamel daily while nourishing the interior tubules and mineral matrixes of your teeth! You can help by drinking pure water, eating pesticide-free and mineral rich foods and by remaining pH balanced. (See pH food chart near the end of this book.)

Fresh Water and Healthy Soil are More Valuable than All of the Resources in the World

Eliot Coleman, organic market gardener and farmer, (www.fourseasonfarm.com) teaches 1000's of people natural ways to care for their plants, soil, fresh waterways and airways. He traveled around the world and found low impact ways to grow a sustainable garden or operate a year-round, small food-market farm which makes a fair profit! I discovered his precious ideas after reading that chemical fertilizer run-off was the main culprit fueling blue-green algal blooms in fresh water lakes. Then I read about David Schindler, a professor at the University of Alberta, who has worked four decades on lake ecology and has seen many lakes destroyed by human-caused algal overgrowth. He said a concerted effort must be made from all levels of government to protect Canada's freshwater lakes. Seventy percent of the earth's surface is water and three percent is fresh. One percent is accessible for direct human uses and only this amount, which is found in reservoirs, underground sources, rivers and lakes, is regularly renewed by rain and snowfall, and is therefore available on a sustainable basis. More and more people worldwide know that last century's chemically harmful living and farming cannot continue. Take care of our soil and fresh water or we die too.

I glanced at the lake while walking from my home to a store that just opened in our town. I found it was full of plastics and chemicals and I thought not only ought governments and chemical farmers be called to task but each one of us too. We are all governors of our own homes and lives. Each of us can ask the stores, restaurants, farmers, developers and manufacturers, in a large concerted effort to change and protect soil and fresh water. If we buy chemical foods and items and live in ways which poison and ultimately kill us and our kids, we have no one to blame but ourselves. In the store I saw 1000's of products and only two that cared about the earth. One was made in Canada and printed on it in capital letters was: PRODUCTS THAT LEAVE NO TRACE ON THE EARTH OR ITS INHABITANTS. I bought the two products and left the store. In a sense, each one of the 7,000,000,000 of us is an inspector of our own lives. We decide what we will or will not buy or do. Support the manufacturers, food farmers and stores that provide products that care about soil and fresh water and the life within it because that is care for *you*.

Anti-Stress and Self-Massage

This is a chapter about relaxing with self-massage through-out your day or night rather than waiting until you are depleted or hurt.

Most people, including some medical doctors, do not know the depth of the healing power we have within us when we use stress releasing care, like self-massage. Stress can act as a motivator or energizer, yet too much bad stress can cause problems as your body responds physically. Overwork, exhaustion, unresolved frustration, or concerns during your day can cause all sorts of physical, mental, or emotional tensions to build up in your body.

The following tips can calm, soothe, release, heal and relax you as you realign your muscles and ligaments, improve your mood, and reconnect with your soul! Additional benefits are that you can learn more about your body, improve your flexibility (which can help prevent injuries), improve circulation and oxygenation, and balance your nervous system. You may enjoy doing these tips each day or in bed at night several times a week. Because of the many stressful irritants that can go unnoticed as you move along in your day, don't be surprised if you find various areas of your body that are tense, sore, and painful and more than ready for your relieving care.

Lift Up from Your Heart

Have you ever been told to stop slouching and immediately stood up stiffly at attention and threw your shoulders back? Instead, stand relaxed and lift up from your heart. Imagine that you have a string starting at your heart area and running up out of the top of your head. Now imagine taking your hand and pulling that string which runs from your heart to the top of your head. Tug gently up and feel your spine elongate and your pelvis drop down into natural alignment, head, heart, spine, pelvis, powerfully (yet not stiff) back to where they belong.

Work out your facial muscles

For a happy relaxed face and neck try this:

- Wiggle your nose.
- Lift your forehead and eyebrows up high and hold for three seconds.
- With two or three fingers, push on your cheeks and smile widely as your cheek muscles touch against your fingers. Smile and release several times.
- Shape your lips like a small "o" as if you are ready to give someone a kiss on the cheek. Then quickly smile instead. Do this three times.
- First warn your family that you are fine. Then, raise your eyebrows high as you can, open your eyes wide and grimace at the same moment.
- While relaxing in a comfy chair lean back and look up at the ceiling puckering your lips. Then soften your mouth and stick your relaxed tongue out as far as possible and gently move your neck around to de-stress your neck muscles. It works!
- Everyone should be wide eyed or snickering by now, so open your lips wide like an enormous "O" and then stick your relaxed tongue out as far as you can and hold for three seconds.

To finish take a big breath. Can you feel the increased circulation in your face and the relaxation in your jaw and neck?

The Sacred Towel

This towel pain relief technique may well be the reason that Douglas Adams, author of the book *Hitchhikers Guide to the Galaxy*, included the towel as one of the main character's essential galaxy travel items.

This tip requires a rolled up towel that you will use under your low back and your neck. Carefully roll up a small or large towel, choosing the size based on your body shape. Use some string or large elastic bands to secure the rolled towel.

Lie down on a sofa, on the floor on a rug, or on your bed if it is time to sleep, and place the rolled towel underneath the curve of your back releasing tension as your back muscles rest for sixty seconds. Next, move the towel to beneath your neck letting those hard working muscles relax. Finally, lie with the length of your spine right on top of the rolled towel and for seconds (or more) allow your spine to elongate as any tight muscles let go. If you like, roll up three towels of different lengths or sizes to support your hard working neck, spine, and back all at the same time. For a towel massage, move your body gently back and forth while lying on the towel rolls in order to reach deeper and release tight or painful areas.

Symbolically Climbing a Tree

When I was a little girl, I used to climb trees. It was fun and it naturally stretched my arms and legs. Now, as I've gotten older, I still imagine that I am climbing tree branches when I get off my chair at the end of a long day. I stretch my arms up above my head as I come off my chair lifting my legs as if I am climbing a tree.

Try this for ten seconds right now. Stand up and figuratively climb and play. If others are watching you, it will be great fun for them, and if they want to be alive and well in this increasingly technological world and they're smart and love having a well body, they'll join you!

Feel that wonderful stretching in your arms, legs, neck, and spine. If you are accustomed to climbing and can strongly support yourself, find a real tree or playground—and climb!

Bouncing on the Balance Ball Supported by the Big Ball (Earth)

I grew up not realizing that I was standing on a magnificent ball called planet Earth. These exercises involve a balance or exercise ball, which is like a big, thick colorful balloon that will hold your weight. You can purchase one inexpensively at your local sport or health store.

You can sit and bounce on it, flop down on it face down on your tummy, or lean with your back on it. You can be still or you can roll here and there on it and release every muscle of your body. Most of these balls come with instructions and tips, but the most important thing is to listen to your body and what it needs after you get on the ball!

Shoulder Self-Massage

As a young woman I lived and worked on a horse farm and we worked very hard. No one ever told me that after a long day I could do self-massage, reaching my sore muscles and kneading for relief. Instead, I took a painkiller! Thank goodness I have learned how to self-massage and I am happy to share it with you now so you don't have to take a pill! Whether you have tight shoulders, aches, pains, blocks, or tension, giving yourself a light or deep tissue massage anywhere you hurt is very beneficial to your body and can help you relax.

Take a moment now and place your right hand on the top muscle near your left shoulder, kneading your muscles for six to ten seconds. Then, reverse it and do the other side. Take a deep breath and release your grasp. You can do this with any set of muscles including your thighs, calves, upper and lower arms, and your sides. You can use your fingers to make light surface strokes to calm and soothe fiery nerves.

Incredible Hulk Turns Belly Dancer

Incredible Hulk was an animated character that had huge stiff looking muscles. So how do you go from that to looking like a relaxed belly dancer whose muscles move in a very fluid manner? If Sore or Stiff is your middle name, here is a powerful, fun way you can become more flexible. Find a comfortable place in a room that is large enough for you to move about. Sway back and forth gently and stretch your arms out. Let your hands and wrists move easily in small circles. Every part of your body has the ability to flow, so move in a way you didn't know it could—and giggle a lot.

Next, move your body like smaller to larger waves in the ocean. With your hands and arms, be like the wind with laughing curls separating the waves. Soon your body's inner ocean will be moving about in circles, waving, and flowing. These movements help to lubricate your joints, tendons, muscles, and to increase flow and relaxation within your body-ocean.

Give Me Five

Remember gym class? The teacher would say give me five laps. Give me five push-ups. When you feel stiff or achy or have been sitting at technology too long, give yourself five, right on the spot. I just did five push-ups on the kitchen floor as my tea water heated. Then I did one lap around the house as my tea steeped. Now, I'm back sitting very still typing at my computer chair. Start seeing the walls, stairs, or carpet of your office or home as a place to do five push-ups or stretches. Can you see how giving yourself five, here and there throughout the day, can work for you beautifully between everything else you have to do?

Release Tense Upper Body Muscles

The upper body muscles can remain as tight as a drum even as you sleep, after a day of holding your head up. If you are home, consider trying this releasing position if it feels right for you.

Lie down lengthwise on the sofa or you can use a balance ball. With your upper back supported against the sofa arm (or you can do this on a bed or the floor), move yourself into a comfortable knees up, feet flat on the floor, fully supported position.

Gently lift your body up just a wee bit putting a little pressure on the back of your upper body for six to ten seconds. Feel the support of your feet and the sofa (floor or ball) beneath you. Take in a few deep breaths. Do this a few times raising up higher or wiggling around a bit to relax and rest your upper back muscles.

1-2-3 *Self-Massage*

Take three to five minutes to give yourself quick but a calming and rejuvenating whole body massage. Like a traveler treading lightly, exploring the mountains of the Earth, use your hands to travel over and soothe your achy muscles, nerves and skin.

1) Start at your face, resting your palms over your eyes for ten to sixty seconds. Then gently move your fingers firmly in a circular motion calming over your forehead, cheeks, and jaw. Holding your neck pull your fanned fingers forward relaxing both sides of your neck.

2) Continue using your palms and fingers to apply pressure in sweeping circular motions. Soothe the skin of your collarbones, the top and front of your shoulders, your throat, sternum, and chest. Press your fingers over your ribs, tummy, and sides, reaching as far onto your back as you can, then knead over your hips, buttocks, and the front and back of your thighs and calves.

3) With a gentle pinching and squeezing motion massage over your feet and toes and then give each of your arms, hands, and fingers the same ache relieving care.

Pain in the Neck Massage

To release your hard-working achy steel-belted neck, choose one side of your neck and begin. Using your thumb and fingers opposite that side, lightly grasp, squeezing up and down the long tight neck muscles that lie there. Get a firm, yet gentle grip and continue to move up and down massaging along the neck muscle for ten to thirty seconds. Lean your head away from the side you are working on to further help you to get a better hold. At first, if your muscles feel tight, give them time to recognize what is happening. Don't stop. Take a few deep breaths as you feel your neck muscles relaxing and lengthening.

Laundry Dance of Veils

In my adult life, after years of doing repetitive household chores, I found a way to use my imagination to incorporate body care: While doing laundry I relieve my tight shoulders or stiff neck by grasping some clothing from time to time and dancing across the floor with them in each hand. Whirling for a moment around the room I do "the dance of seven veils." (Okay, it was the dance of seven pair of boxers!)

One to Ten Self-Massage

Take ten minutes to give yourself a whole body, deep self-massage. Before going to sleep, upon awakening, or during a bath are good times to do this:
1) Place your palms over your eyes and take a deep breath.
2) Breathing normally gently massage your face with your fingertips, using up and down or circular strokes.
3) Lightly scratch your head all over.
4) Use up and down, circular, or kneading strokes to smooth your neck and upper chest muscles, arm muscles, then the ligaments and joints of your hands and fingers.
5) Use large circular motions on your torso, stomach, and hips. Apply more circular pressure on any tight spots.
6) Bring your knees to your chest and use the heel of your palms to knead the thigh muscles, front and back. Or, sit up and lean over your thighs to massage them.
7) With bent knees or sitting up and bending over your thighs, use up and down finger sweeps and kneading finger motions over your calves.
8) Apply circular strokes with your thumbs on the muscles, tendons, and joints of your ankles, top of feet, soles, and toes.
9) Do your best to reach and massage your back and the back of your hips and tailbone, in any way you are comfortable.
10) Pull your knees to your chest and hug them for ten seconds. Take a big breath.

You will find that your body will tell you what it needs each time you offer an ache and tension melting self-care massage.

Front-Back Switch Self-Massage

For many years I've tried to find a way to reach my back in order to massage it and release sore muscles after a hard day of work. I can now reach anywhere with self-massage and have finally figured out how to massage my back. (I do it physically, yet also energetically!) It is my pleasure to share these three tips with you:

1) Place your back on a corner of a wall. Like a bear using a tree to scratch, lean in and massage away!

2) Place two tennis balls into a long sock. Holding the top of the sock behind you, lean against a wall and the balls and roll away back aches and tension. (You can also lie on the floor with the ball-sock under your back and feel wonderful back releases.)

3) You can use your mind's eye to energetically dissolve back muscle tightness or pain. Give your chest, sternum, ribs, and Adam's apple some gentle self-massage, but, while doing this, also use your imagination to tune in to your back to *melt* the muscles of your back, shoulders, and spine. Imagine you are able to reach right through from front to back with energetic fingers. "See" yourself massaging and releasing every inch of tension from your own back. The cellular and life energy (or chi) throughout your body are connected, which means that your back will respond to your *intent* to bring care to it.

Do Nothing

How would it feel to take an hour for *you* to do mindless, body-resting, music listening, candle lit, soothing nothing? Take ten to sixty second moments to breathe, stretch and rest your eyes daily. Sometimes you might need more time. Find an hour comfortably in your day or evening and do mindless nothing just for you! Watch how your energy rises. Watch how you become balanced in restful beautiful nothing. Enjoy!

> I wonder when in our infinite history
> and on which planet in the universe
> the concept of peace originated,
> for that matter where it still exists,
> that we might be reminded of its particular kind of bliss.
> —Marilyn Idle

Your Armchair Zen Garden

A traditional Zen garden consists of a pit of sand or gravel with carefully placed rock. The sand is artfully raked daily in patterns that evoke the ripples of the sea. You can create your own mini Zen garden by filling a bowl with sand, placing tiny rocks in it and raking the sand to your heart's content. While a tiny Zen garden may not bring about the deep meditation a real Japanese rock garden will, it may provide a little bit of the calming you need to get through the day.

Enjoy this peaceful place during the ups and downs and ebbs and flows of your life.

Relaxing Home Spa

This is a chapter about giving yourself soothing luxurious moments with easy home-spa self-care

If someone had told me years ago that I could have amazing relaxation spa moments for myself at home or that I was a self-healer or that my natural state was peace, calm, and wellness, I wouldn't have believed them. With the overabundance of painkillers, expensive technology, doctors doing medical diagnostics, poised with scalpels to replace joints and other body parts  with metal or plastic implants, you won't blame me for not knowing that simple daily self-care would be what actually helped me remain well!

Spas around the world offer talks on their methods of natural care and wellness. So similarly, pick up an inspirational book and read a little during a soak or afterward when you are resting. Spa-time is not just "girl-time", the guys enjoy it too! Your mini at-home spa days are about experiencing love and kindness for yourself. If you invite friends or family members to do the same, they can feel your self-love, as you extend it to them.

Quiet Time

You don't have to go to a meditation retreat to be quiet, sit on a rug, breathe deeply, or to repeat your favorite mantra. Sit for a few minutes and notice what is going on inside of you. Watch your thoughts as if they were beautiful birds flying by, or landing and resting in a tree.

If You Can't Eat or Drink It, Don't Put It on Your Skin

Whether it is a soothing body cream or cleansing scrub, if you wouldn't eat it, then don't put it on your skin! One of the easiest at-home spa treatments is to prepare a homemade body scrub, apply it, and then take a hot bath. Or take a bath with sea or mineral salt, which can be found at your health food store. Even a bath with a different than you normally use luxurious, natural soap, or organic shower gel is a treat. Here are some homemade body scrubs:

Cocoa Skin Smoother

To eliminate rough areas on your feet, mix five tablespoons of cocoa powder with water to obtain a thick paste. Apply on clean and dry feet, cover with old cotton socks and leave it on for twenty to thirty minutes. Afterwards, wash away.

Coffee Exfoliation Scrub

Exfoliate means to scrub away lifeless or clogged surface skin on your face or body. Organic coffee works well for this. First, in a bowl, blend:

2 cups of coarsely ground organic fair trade coffee
½ cup sea salt or raw sugar
2 to 3 tablespoons cold pressed almond oil (or any fresh oil you enjoy eating and have on hand)

Now, step into a hot shower. After your skin is moistened and your pores open, using fingers in large circular motions, massage the coffee scrub onto your skin with firm even pressure. Leave it on for several minutes enjoying the steam of the shower, while staying out of the direct stream of water. If you enjoy the heavenly coffee aroma, you could put the plug in and let the tub fill and then bathe in the coffee before you rinse it off. Or just rinse and then step out of the shower and pat your skin gently dry. For a protective finish to your silky skin, smooth on a thin layer of your favorite organic body lotion.

Don't Eat Sugar, Scrub and Exfoliate Your Face or Body with It!

Sugar is acidic and a great facial exfoliate because it tends not to irritate your skin. When lifeless skin clogs or collects on the surface of your face, it's important to slough it away. When skin isn't exfoliated, it can sometimes appear dry. Facial exfoliates also help to clear up clogged pores. For normal or mature skin blend in a bowl:

Two tablespoons sugar and three tablespoons warm water. Make sure to stir the sugar long enough so that it melts, as granules not dissolved could scratch your skin. Apply this to your face and gently massage around your skin for one to three minutes. Splash your face with warm water or use a warm wet washcloth to rinse.

Honey, Sugar, Soft Skin

Soft skin is an invitation to cuddle. Well, anything is an invitation to cuddle for me! This soft skin formula is an exfoliant and skin moisturizing treatment. Blend in a bowl:

½ cup of fair trade raw turbinado cane sugar (or brown sugar)
¼ cup of honey
Add some essential oil to make it smell even lovelier. Try lavender or rose, both edible flowers. Or, try a touch of citrus such as lime or tangerine.

Begin by running a bath or starting the shower. Standing in the tub or just out of the stream of the shower, use gloves or a face cloth to smooth this blend over your whole body. Put more pressure on rough areas such as your heels, knees, or elbows, and in cellulite areas such as the thighs and buttocks. Cellulite is fatty deposits under your skin that sometimes hold metabolic or environmental toxins especially if you wear a lot of tight clothing that limits lymph drainage.

Now is the perfect time to gently release them and wash them away with water. Your skin will glow and feel really soft. Rest afterwards. Apply organic body lotion or cream over your whole body immediately after the shower to moisturize.

Give Yourself an Easy Facial

Prepare a small amount of fresh facemask and homemade moisturizer using the recipes below. You may already have many of the ingredients in your own kitchen. Improvise with what you have on hand. When you have the mask mixture made, set a fluffy towel nearby and prepare a basin of hot water. Place a drop or two of your favorite essence oil in it if you like. Let the steam ease the pores of your skin open, your face about three inches above the basin for three minutes. Drape a towel over your head to keep the steam in like a sauna. Breath, relax, enjoy.

Next, apply the mask to your skin. Leave it on for three to ten minutes. Then remove with a splash of water or a cloth. Finish by cleansing your face soothingly with natural organic gel or soap, rinse, pat your face gently dry and apply a thin layer of moisturizer.

Note: If you have oily or acne prone skin, mud or clay-based masks are great for balancing your skin. Dry skin will benefit from hydrating masks made from glycerine, honey, and oils. Green tea masks are great for soothing the skin. Masks can be kept on for three to ten minutes.

The Rose Facial

This homemade facial or body mask is wonderful for balancing out the oily and dry areas of your skin. Use:

6 fresh rose petals (optional)
2 tablespoons rosewater (available from internet or health stores)
1 tablespoon natural organic yogurt, room temperature (not non-fat)
1 tablespoon smooth honey (to change hard honey into liquid honey warm it on low heat in a little pot for a minute)

Soak the rose petals in a touch of pure water and then mash them in the bowl. Add the rosewater, yogurt, and honey.

Mix well and gently massage onto your face. Leave on for three to six minutes or longer and then rinse and lightly pat your face dry.

Facial Mask for Sensitive or Sunburned Skin

This is a simple, pure, and soothing mask made in your kitchen. Blend in a bowl:

1 cup natural organic plain yogurt
½ cup organic oatmeal (quick oatmeal or ground oatmeal works well)

Then, gently massage the mask onto your face using circular strokes with your fingers. Let it nourish your skin for six to ten minutes and then wash off with a washcloth and warm water.

Moisturizing Scary Green Face Mask

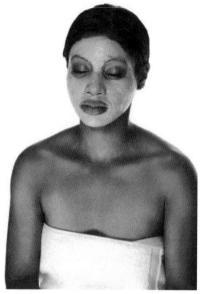

Avocados and honey are exceptionally moisturizing. This mask is particularly great for mature, wrinkled, and dry skin. Use a ripe, fresh, organic ½ avocado and mix it with ¼ cup of honey. Make sure to mash it up into a creamy paste. This is the classic "scary green mask" recipe for dry skin. Gently massage onto your face and leave for six to ten minutes, then rinse with a cool washcloth. This mask is great for soothing sunburned, winter or wind chapped, or otherwise irritated skin. It works well for moisturizing other skin types as well: For oily skin, mix in a couple more drops of lemon or lime juice; for dry skin, mix in a couple more tablespoons of honey.

Homemade Moisturizers

Here are several simple homemade cream recipes for your face and body. These homemade lotions are affordable, effective and best for your body because they are fresh and you know the ingredients. You can find the oils on the Internet or at health stores. Make sure the oils smell fresh. Keep all but the portion you're going to use immediately, in the refrigerator.

Day Moisturizer for Normal Skin

Pour into a glass bottle and blend together:

4 tablespoons sweet almond oil
Add your favorite essential oil fragrance or this flowery combination:
10 drops lavender
10 drops lemon oil
10 drops chamomile blue
30 drops rose

Massage a few drops of this moisturizer daily into your washed and slightly damp face or onto your body. Then pat away excess with a clean tissue.

Day or Night Moisturizer for Normal, Sensitive or Mature Skin

This beautiful face cream is perfect for every type of skin. Over very low heat in a pot, melt the oils and wax very slowly, stirring all the time.

6 tablespoons apricot kernel oil
6 tablespoons avocado oil
6 tablespoons sweet almond oil
6 tablespoons beeswax
6 tablespoons rosewater

Take off heat as soon as it is melted. Add rosewater and beat well until cool and nice and smooth. Pour into a glass jar.

Coconut Moisturizer

This is a tropical treat for your face. In a pot over very low heat, heat all ingredients until warm. Pour into a glass jar and shake well before each use.

6 teaspoons cold pressed coconut oil
2 teaspoons organic safflower or almond oil
1 teaspoon lemon juice
1 teaspoon lime juice
10 drops or lavender or rose or your favorite essential oil (optional)

This cream can be used over your entire body and face. Massage it gently into your skin using circular motions. It takes a moment or two until it absorbs into your hands, so enjoy massaging your hard-working fingers. You can store the mixture at room temperature for up to three days or, refrigerated, this moisturizer will last up to two weeks.

Fresh Flower Skin Toner for All Skin Types

After cleansing or masking your face, closing your pores can help protect against environmental irritants, which can cause blemishes or blackheads. Other benefits of using toner include increased circulation to the skin, improved skin tone, and reduction of lines and wrinkles. Astringents draw water from the underlying skin to the surface, which results in nourishment, cleansing, and smaller lines and pores. Store-bought facial toners often contain chemicals, which swell skin by causing irritation and inflammation. While they close pores and cause the illusion of reduced wrinkles, they can be harmful if used over long periods of time, and they can *cause* dry and flaking skin. By making this flower toner or other natural facial toner at home, you can use nourishing herbs specific to your skin-care needs and no harmful ingredients will be absorbed into your skin!

Make a tea of camomile, thyme, and lavender flowers. Strain it into a glass jar and allow it to cool. This flower facial toner is good for all skin types. The ingredients are easy to grow in your garden, or you can buy them dried at your local health food store. Apply this tea to your face with a cotton ball to remove excess cleanser and to close the pores after washing. This will keep your skin clean and clear with regular use.

Just Water Skin Toner!

Although herbal natural facial toner offers a way to pamper your skin as part of regular skin-care, plain cold water is also a great toner. This is an excellent care after you do a mini at-home facial. Gently apply cold water with an organic cotton ball or soft cloth on your face.

Tea Bath to Soothe Sunburn

If you prefer to not use sunscreens but have accidentally stayed out too long in the sun, try this: You will need a towel, six to ten bags of organic black tea, and a double batch of the above mask for sensitive or sunburned skin.

After you have made the soothing mask, place a large fluffy soft towel next to your bath. While you fill your bath about a quarter to halfway full with cool water, make a very strong pot of fair trade organic black tea. Add the tea to your bath water and lie in the tub and soak for ten minutes or more. Making sure you have a non-slip mat in place, carefully stand up and soothe the cream all over the sunburned areas of your body. Leave it on for three to six minutes, or less time if you feel too cool to stand any longer. Rinse off and gently dab your skin dry with a soft towel.

Next time when you have had enough sun, you can protect your skin by retreating under a shady tree, opening your umbrella, or wearing a big hat and a long sleeved, thin, cotton shirt.

A Soak for Your Hands

Prepare a bowl for your hands by filling with very warm water, plus a few drops of rose water, or lemon or lime juice. If you want to make it very special add some skin soothing marigold or rose petals, put on your favorite soothing music and light a candle. Prepare a cup of herbal tea or pour your favorite drink to have nearby. Soak your hands for six to ten minutes. After you rinse your hands and dry them, apply a few drops of a nutritive oil such as cold pressed almond, apricot, cold pressed coconut oil and add, if you have it, a few drops of vitamin E (you may simply break a vitamin E capsule).

Massage this precious oil into your cuticles, wrap your hands in a small towel and leave it on for three to six minutes. Now push the cuticles with a nail stick and file your nails to your favorite shape. If your nails and hands crack easily, especially with household chores, gardening, or in the winter, do the treatment once a week if you want healthy, strong nails and smooth, crack-free fingers and hands.

Massage Your Hands

I can't believe how much computers have changed how I use my fingers, hands, and arms! Our hands and fingers work as hard as the rest of our bodies and can carry a lot of tension. You can start by loving and thanking your arms, hands, and fingers, then massaging! Breathe deeply a couple of times and then breathe normally throughout this hand massage. You can massage your hands dry, or put on a tiny amount of organic lotion.

Hold your hand and begin stroking the back, pushing gently yet firmly above your wrists and gliding up your arm. Let your fingers slide back smoothly to the tips of your fingers. Press between the tendons on the back of your hand with your fingers. Do three strokes in each furrow on the top of your hand, continuing past the wrists and a little way up your arm. Now, turn your hand over and cup it under the hand you're massaging. Knead your whole palm using circular pressure with your thumb and forefinger. Continue past your wrist and up your arm, then go up and down each finger individually using circular pressure, kneading around the joints.

To finish, gently squeeze the skin between each finger. Then hold each finger and very gently give it a slow tug, stretching it long and holding it for a second or two. Then lightly shake and move each joint of each finger moving from base to tip. End by applying a little more soothing organic hand lotion.

Foot Bath and Massage at Your Home Mini-Spa

Our wonderful feet take us everywhere. Some days we can be on them, pounding the pavement the whole day, yet scarcely take a moment to care for them. Here's how to care for them and your feet will love you for it!

If you have time, first run a little warm water into your bathtub or into a smaller tub that is big enough to fit both of your feet into. (If you don't have time, do the three-minute mini-foot massage below.) Add a drop of something soothing like rose or lavender flower essence. If you have rose petals from your garden you can put them into the water. If you need to release soreness, add ¼ cup Epsom salts, baking soda, or sea salt. Soak, soak, and soak! Rinse your feet gently. Pat them dry, and dry between each toe.

Start your three-minute, refreshing mini foot massage by taking a deep relaxing breath. Then hold your foot and knead it with small circular motions. Massage each toe. Press between the tendons on the top of your foot. Massage each joint and pull gently on each toe. To finish, give some squeezes to each foot. And then smooth on some soothing, peppermint foot lotion.

Late Night Quickie Foot Massage

Sometimes late in the evening I need self-care and I would love to do a pampering foot massage but it is too late for a spa moment. So, I get ready for sleep, quickly wash my feet with a hot soapy cloth, rinse and dry. I crawl into bed and take a big relaxing breath while pulling my knees to my chest and wrapping my arms to hug them for a back releasing stretch. Then I reach for one foot and then the other giving each foot top, ankle, sole and toe a small peppermint foot lotion massage!

Release Your Breasts and Keep Them Wonderfully Well with Self-Care!

There are many things you can do to protect the healthy flow and wellness of your breasts, the precious heart center and nurturing area of your body. First, the skin of our breasts actually provides a natural *bra*, and it is healthy to wear only that as often as possible. Consume only fresh chemical-free food and drink as much as possible. Do light tissue, lymph-draining self-massage for sixty seconds before you go to sleep at night, or during your bath or shower. Use homemade masks on your breasts, which can improve waste elimination, maintain elasticity, and support cell regeneration.

Our breasts are primarily fatty tissue and the pectoral muscles give support. Keeping breasts sealed tightly for too long a period in a bra can impair lymph system flow and create an accumulation of stagnant materials within breast tissue. The cells can become oxygen-starved or over-acidified with wastes. In simple terms, the fatty tissue and cells can then become weakened, over-replicate in lower level "gasping for life" impaired functioning, which is sometimes medically called cancer. Really common sense tells us that a dis-eased body condition, most often caused by a lack of care, nurturance, cleansing, nourishment, and a need for balancing. Cancer, the monster disease, is a condition that is a result of being out of balance: when you rebalance, there won't be any malfunctioning cells in you!

Soothe Your Eyes with an Eye Pack

Eye packs are small pillows you put over your eyes to relax and soothe you before sleep at night or if your eyes are irritated. Buy or make your own eye pack and put it on your eyes for three minutes or more. The weight of it alone is so relaxing—and if you add lavender, even more so. Eye packs should weigh about one pound. They can be used cool or cold. Eye packs are ideal to have anywhere you go for a quick soothe during or after a day of hard work, or when your eyes are tired. You might find it hard to believe that a simple eye pack can give your eyes such amazing comfort, refreshment, and soothing results as they do. I love them so much that I made dozens for family and friends. Then they started making them for their family and friends.

Here's how to make eye packs at home. You will need a piece of raw silk or cotton material about twelve inches long and six inches wide. It can be a rectangular shape or you can be creative and cut out an oval mask shape. Sew the sides leaving a small break so you can fill it up when you're done. Turn it inside out and fill it with, about one pound of organic, fair trade rice or flax seeds; two tablespoons of lavender buds or more; twenty drops of lavender oil.

Stitch your eye pack tightly closed. Put it in a plastic bag in the freezer and take it out when you are ready to use it. After use, seal it in the bag again and let it stay in the freezer unless you prefer room temperature. The ones I made have lasted for years. To keep the surface clean, I made eye-pillow slips to slide onto the eye pack before use.

Cool Your Aching Skin with Water

At-home, or even adapted for work, your mini spa can relieve aches and help you feel refreshed, cared for, and well. A cooling cloth removes inflammation from your hurting neck. So during your day, as needed, keep a simple wet cloth nearby. Imagine—rather than numbing with painkillers, you can dissolve pain or stiffness in your neck and face in a moment or two using a warm or cold cloth.

No matter how much work you have to do, if you are feeling tired or hurting, *stop* for one to three minutes. That is just enough time to fill a sink, wet your face, and dip your aching hands or feet into warm or cool healing water or wipe your brow with a warm or cold cloth.

Maintain a Youthful Outer Appearance by Nourishing "Inside"

As a teen, I lived on junk food and that took its toll. My body was constantly acting like it had a "flu or cold". Yet now I know the acne, aches, pains, stuffiness and uncomfortable symptoms, most often, were inflammation. My body was simply eliminating and cleansing.

Proper nutrition is of utmost importance to maintain *you*. Daily adequate movement, healthy eating and a good night's sleep results in the best renewal and maintenance of your body's cells and skin. That in turn makes you feel and look young.

Munch on a few raw nuts, hemp seeds, pumpkin or sunflower seeds, as they are good for you "on the inside". These are a rich source of essential fatty acids which support cell, nerve and brain function and can also prevent hair loss. They give you radiant skin, flexible tough fingernails and uplift your heart and immune system. No matter what else you may eat be sure to add plenty of fresh organic or spray-free vegetables and fruits to your diet as they are rich in water, fiber and nutrients and contribute to the healthy regeneration and happy functioning of your body and skin. Sorry to be the bearer of sad news ... steer clear of over-loading on junk food and processed sugar, as these are the main culprits of aging and aging-related diseases. If you do indulge (and who doesn't?), simply support your body to cleanse before going to sleep, by drinking some lemon water, going for a three minute walk for fresh air or doing a few push-ups on the stairs.

Jump in the Sea Tonight

Here is a way to say "I love you" to your body for all it endures and does. Give yourself a wonderful ocean-like bath. Put two cups of sea salt, baking soda, or Epsom salts into a bathtub full of water and jump in! Enjoy a fifteen-minute soak. Rinse yourself with fresh warm water before you step out of the tub! This will soothe away pains, and the warm comfort just before going to bed can help you sleep more deeply and peacefully.

Calming Stretches

This is a chapter about the ease and importance of bringing short and simple stretches into your day.

Millions of people have experienced the drug-free health benefits of stretching. If I had known that stretching (even for three minutes a day) felt so good, that it really doesn't *feel like* exercise, and that it was natural and so much fun, I would have started doing it years ago! Now, I stretch as unsurprisingly as a cat anytime, anywhere, and whenever I need to throughout my day! Stretching is innate, yet many of us rarely do it anymore. Your body will stretch often and as easily as your heart beats and you breathe, but only *if* you are not programmed to be too stiff and socially correct in your movement.

I know from experience that if I have my body working at one angle or position for a long time, or do repetitive actions like keyboarding or gaming, it can cause symptoms of actual premature aging! Loss of flexibility and calcium deposits or lactic acid build up in tissues can occur. Metabolic waste bi-products and oxygen-starvation in your cells make your muscles feel achy. Also dehydration in connective tissue can change the chemical structure of the tissues, especially if you eat a lot of sugary treats or drink acidic beverages like cola or coffee, which are irritating and inflaming, as opposed to alkaline foods and fresh water that cool and soothe you.

Until your body re-learns to naturally stretch again in response to aches or stiffness, keeping yourself moving and doing short reaching, bending, and twisting stretches is the most powerful way to recover ease, flexibility, comfort, and keep a healthy range of motion. Naturally calming stretches also elongate connective tissues, soothe nerves, relieve muscle tension, help eliminate waste and water retention while bringing more circulation, and therefore oxygen, to your tissues.

Here are some stretching refreshers to help bring natural movement and a deeper state of relaxation back to your neck, arms, chest, torso, and legs—your whole body! It is never too late to re-learn to stretch and you can do it anytime and anywhere you desire. Be patient as you learn the simple stretches to get you going and help you remain flexible and feel good, for the rest of your life. Remember self-care is about listening to yourself and the clues from your body because with your attention your body will let you know what to do!

Here are some ideas to get you started:

Get up and fly like an Irish River Dancer skipping and dancing across the floor like there's no tomorrow. Do a self-hug or a back arching cat stretch before you get out of your car after you arrive at your destination. Do a seat-wiggling dance while sitting at your desk or watching a movie. Do a waist twist while standing in line at the supermarket or theatre. Two of the most effective and relaxing places to stretch and release tension from your body are in a hot bath or just before sleep under the covers in your cozy, warm bed. You get the idea, anytime and anyplace is a good time to stretch!

PC Keyboard and Game Users

When we work at our computers or play with computerized games, most of us tend to get into frozen body positions and to limit our movements. This can lead to repetitive strain injuries accompanied by pain or numbness. Every thirty minutes or so do a chair-dance! Push yourself well back from your keyboard (or move completely away) and move your arms, head, and body all around. Every sixty minutes let yourself fall onto the floor or lean your back against the wall to stretch and soothe your muscles. During your work hours, move around on your chair. Become that kid that endlessly dismayed the classroom teachers—the wiggler! Do body shifts from sitting to standing, pelvic tilts, and arms up and out stretches throughout your workday. As often as you push your save button, make a stretching movement to keep you and your beautiful body relaxed, refreshed, flowing, and happy.

Pretzel Twist

While standing or sitting, very slowly sway and twist to the right and to the left. Then, to have a deep upper arm stretch, raise both of your arms and point your hands toward the ceiling. Bend one arm and place your hand on your back. Hold that elbow with the other hand. Twist right and left and then lean slowly to each side. Change arms and repeat. To get a deeper stretch while doing this, casually turn your head to look over your shoulder for a few seconds, as if you were trying to see a friend who is behind you. Repeat on your other side.

Stuffy Office Stretching Tricks

If you have to stand and sit properly in your suit and not stretch or wiggle around to ease tension or stiffness, here are some fun ideas to get you to a location where you can have a stretch moment. Take an extra bathroom break, even when you don't have to "go" so you can really stretch and refresh. Step outside to get that thing you "forgot." Look out a window at the sky with an "I am really thinking about this" look on your face. Your body will let you know all sorts of ways to become a natural stretcher again.

Baby Moves

If you are constantly working on a keyboard or have body stiffness or weakness from sitting and working in one position for too long, consider learning about and then doing regenerative exercises called Somatics and Pilates. For me Somatics helps me release muscles which are stiff from repetitive use and Pilates builds core muscle strength. I call these techniques "baby moves" because they resemble natural movements made by infants, babies and toddlers who are rolling about, reaching out, lifting their necks or crawling in order to build strength and to learn how to move their limbs and bodies in a strong, co-ordinated way.

Giraffe Stretch

Sitting with your neck crunched forward, with your arms on the keyboard, can constrict your neck and throat. It can also tense up your eyes, skull, and jaw. If this is you, reach up and self-massage your jaw, while faking a yawn. Then lift your neck long like a giraffe. Breathe normally and feel the tension melting away in your throat. If you need some bigger body movements, go get a glass of water to cool your throat during the releases.

Cat Claw Stretch for Hands and Fingers

While taking a deep breath, stretch your arms in front of you like a cat. Reaching out, do a claws-out stretch, spreading your fingers and flexing and closing them a few times. Then, breathing deeply then normally again, drop your arms to your sides and shake out your shoulders, hands, and fingers for three to six seconds to finish.

Get Un-Nerved

Here is a really nice stretch for releasing pressure on the buttocks, hips, and sciatic nerve area. The sciatic nerve begins in the lower back and runs through your tailbone, buttocks, and hip area, then down each of your lower limbs. If over-pressured from sitting too much it can cause a shooting throbbing pain down your legs. When any muscles or nerves of your body are overused or pressured for too long, especially if you ignore the initial tired-tight-please-stretch-or-rest-response, they can become persistently achy. When you get that first indication of sciatica pain, listen to it! Stand up for a few seconds and sway your hips for a bit. If you have persistent pain in your buttock-hip area, there may be inflammation of the nerve. If this is the case:

Lie on your side, legs together and toes pointing down. Prop yourself on your elbow, or put a pillow under you head. Steadying yourself, bring your top leg all the way to the front of you and rock it gently forward. Then bring your top leg all the way to the back as far as you can comfortably draw it behind you.

Doing this daily stretch will ease pressure and tightness allowing refreshing circulation. Do both sides of your body and it will help your muscles and nerves remember their natural relaxed and free flowing state and your buttocks' nerves will thank you too!

Opening and Closing an Imaginary Jar

This tip will help you remember to relax and stretch your arms and hands during and after repetitive typing or video game playing. When you are sitting for too long your upper body and spine become squished down by gravity and shaped like an *S*. Free yourself with this. Lift up and be an *I* not an *S*. Hang your arms down to your sides and loosen your wrists. Whirl your fingers and palms like you are opening and closing a jar several times, first with a slow motion, then medium, and finally a fast motion for about three to six seconds or until you feel comfortable to stop.

Now, point one arm firmly forward, straight in front of you. Take hold of the fingers of that arm with your other hand and pull down gently while resisting, then gently shake your wrist up and down, like the wagging tail of a happy dog. Then do the same to your other arm.

Adam's Apple Breath

For an interesting releasing breath, put your tongue behind your front teeth with your mouth gently closed. Then, breathe through your nose, softening and opening your throat. If it is very tight or tender, self-massage gently, pulling the skin near your Adam's apple. Then again, mouth still closed, let your breath come through your nose and flow over a more opened throat. Imagine that your tongue has a root connected all the way to your stomach. See your tongue, in your mind's eye, relaxing all the way down to the bottom of your stomach. If it feels good, do this throat opening and rejuvenating breath a few more times and feel the soothing circulation and energy in your throat and whole torso.

Chin Down

Bring your chin down toward your chest and turn your head to touch the left collarbone, then to the heart center and sternum area in the middle, and then the right collarbone area. Breathe and lift your shoulders up and down, holding them near your ears for five seconds and releasing. Place your hand on your head and gently lean your head to each side. Point your arms to the back of you, then bring them forward and wrap them around you again and have a five-second very firm self-hug. Drop you arms to your side, stretch out your fingers, and shake them out one last time before returning to your keyboard. Take several refreshing quick energizing breaths.

Tilt-a-Whirl

Lie down with your back on the floor on a rug or sofa. Bend your knees up. Breathe, knees together, feet flat. Raise your buttocks and press your lower back down. Then, raise your buttocks high enough to press your upper back firmly into the rug or sofa. If you cannot completely lift your buttocks, then tilt your pelvis and alternately press down onto your upper and then lower back. Either way you do it, wiggle around a bit while in position to allow even more tension release and relaxation.

Toes to Your Nose

Sitting in your chair with one foot on the floor, point the other leg and foot out in front of you. Spread your toes and point them toward your nose, then point out again. Do this two or three times, then shake your leg, foot, and toes, like you are trying to shake off a bug. Stretch the other leg the same way. Take a big refreshing breath and feel it going down to your toes.

The Edge of Your Seat

If you sit at your job or at home a lot, then throughout your day, stop for a moment and do this. Move forward on your chair placing your bottom near the front edge and gently lean your head toward the back of your chair. Stretch your legs, feet, and toes way out in front while using the arms of the chair to steady you. Take a deep breath filling your lungs fully and expanding your belly. Imagine your upper and lower back expanding too. Lean all the way back for ten seconds. Lift your arms up to the sky; then reach your arms back behind your head, and stretch. Then bring your arms above your head again and hold them there as you take another deep breath, and let your shoulders settle downward into their sockets. Slowly lower your arms and hands, cradling the back of your neck, and lean back. Then slowly bring your arms down to your sides. Grasp the bottom of your chair to help you slowly sit upright.

To finish, act as if someone is pulling your shoulders back, holding onto your head, and gently pulling you up into a comfortable posture for you. Take three quick breaths to energize before you go back to work.

Buttocks Chair-Dance

There used to be a TV commercial for a salve to relieve aches where a muscular man made his pectoral muscles dance to music. This chair-dance self-care tip is similar: You make your muscles dance and increase circulation to your lower body, hips, and legs. This releasing and rejuvenating move is done while you are sitting at your chair, unless your home or workspace allows you to get up and break into a dance! Read it through first then have fun.

Breathing normally, lean your body to the left to slightly put pressure onto your left thigh and butt cheek. Tense that side of your bottom and upper and lower thigh muscles. Still leaning on your left sit bone, now lengthen your torso and at the same time raise your left shoulder up to your ear and hold for three to six seconds. This makes an elongating waist stretch. Now release the stretch and come back to center. Repeat the sequence on your right side. To finish, come back to center and lean forward onto both your thighs then lift yourself back to sitting. This alternating cheeky chair dance stretches and relaxes your neck, shoulder, thigh and butt muscles after sitting for too long, and can be done without a TV commercial crew filming!

Wave Goodbye and Hug

You can do this arm wave and hug sitting in your chair in sixty seconds (or while lying down in three to six minutes). Read this through first, then, enjoy the release. Wave you arms in the air several times. Now, drop your arms down to your sides and shake them out. Bring both arms over your head pointing to the twelve o'clock position, then slowly, strongly bring them down to the six o'clock position, and repeat this three times. Finish with a full breath, wrap your arms around yourself, and give yourself a firm tension-releasing hug.

Panda Bear Rolls

I love these back-massaging rolls. They are easy to do and will gently massage your back muscles and spine. Get down on the floor on a rug and hug your knees to your chest. Tuck your chin down and roll back and forth and side to side. Do this three times or more.

Fun Moves

This is a chapter about moving more often during your busy or technology filled day—and fun ways to do it!

If it feels fun and doesn't hurt anyone, do it! Make having fun more important to you than your "politically correct" self-image or what other people think!

Upside-Down and Up Against the Wall

This is a great way to release, relax, and energize your neck, back, buttocks, and legs. Lie on the floor and put your seat against the wall, moving your legs toward the ceiling by edging them up along the wall. Point your toes toward the ceiling and release aches and tension for one to three minutes. (Stay and relax your legs and back for three to six minutes if you have been working, standing, or sitting for many more hours than you should have!)

Wall, Post, Tree

All of these can relax your sore back! If you can't go outside to a beautiful tree, then simply find a post or the corner of a wall. Then release your back and neck by leaning against and into the solid object, while taking relaxing breaths. You deserve the relief and you can release and soothe as many times as needed during the day in as little as ten to thirty seconds.

Put Spring in Your Step to Perk Up!

While getting some new tires installed recently, I waited eight hours in a first come first served tire shop. The waiting room had very large windows and I could see how hard the tire installers worked all day in one small spot putting tires on cars, barely stopping to breathe. You can imagine how surprised I was when I noticed that each time they came into the office from the garage with completed work orders they ran! Not just once or twice, but every time! Then, I saw a sign on the wall depicting tire installers in running stance. I thought, "Do they really *make* them run?" This went on all day. Job after job, the installers ran every single time.

At first, I thought the owners of this company must be slave drivers to make their employees run. Were they so worried about their image to the impatient customers watching from the really bad popcorn, coffee, and candy vending waiting room? How could they force these hard-working people to run all day, when they ought to be given some relaxing short breaks!

In the coming days at home, when getting up from my computer, I found myself running in a way similar to the tire installers, lightly, on my toes to my next destination. At first I thought I'd picked up a habit from watching those driven tire workers! However, then it struck me: I felt *better* after running during my breaks from my limited-motion work! I had a new take on what the men and their bodies were possibly doing by running.

To handle their repetitive-motion, close-quarters work, in a cold garage, they were almost flying in between jobs to release muscle tension, to be free, to exercise their arms and legs, to generate heat, return circulation, and oxygenate every part of their hard working bodies!

My work is not strenuous like that of the tired tire workers, yet I learned something from these people who ran between each job. Now when my body is inclined, no matter how short a distance, I run. People may think, "Wow, she's in a hurry," or "What a driven worker she is," as they see me blast away from my computer. However, if you try it, you will feel the wonderful, freeing, and muscle-releasing self-care!

Yawning is Healthy

Many people restrict energy flow through their whole being by unconsciously holding their breath. If you'll let yourself, a small, relaxed yawn can lead to a huge yawn.

Then the door to oxygenating your cells and relaxing yourself is open. I'm not sure why people think yawning is a sign of boredom. A lion sitting in the sun yawning isn't bored, nor is she offended if another large cat yawns nearby. This is nature's simple way of relaxing, releasing, and bringing in more oxygen! Having a big yawning session and a stretch is especially releasing if you have a tendency to unconsciously clench your jaws and tense your shoulders to your ears.

Open your mouth wide while lifting your fingers, arms and shoulders up toward the sky, and fake a yawn. The yawn response may start on its own, or not, yet even a fake yawn is relaxing and almost as oxygenating as a natural yawn. Make sure you

make an audible aaahhheeeooo sound like Tarzan of the Jungle. The sound massages your internal organs and muscles as well. If you like, you can do a lion aaahhheeeoooroarrrrr at the end of your yawn! The vibration of the roar resounds within your body soothing your nervous system, spine, shoulder and back muscles—and if you roar very loudly, your pelvic floor muscles too.

Comfy Cozy Cuddles

Cuddles are warm, caring, fun non-sexual hugs, kisses, physical touches that fill you up with the most scrumptious cared-for and happy feelings. Many people are afraid of these fun ways of touching or caring because they misperceive nurturance for sexuality. If you rarely or never cuddle with your family or pets then take some cuddle-time today, this evening, and in the next few days. For self-cuddles, just curl up in your favorite cozy chair or wrap up in a comforter and cuddle yourself! With your child or partner perhaps you will jump in and sink together into a pile of pillows and blankets. Then love, laugh, hug, lean on each other, and cuddle together.

Who's the Best Hugger?

I give myself a big hug often. Try it! Your hugs are as loving as anyone's. Wrap your arms around yourself. Hold yourself so strongly that even if a hurricane came you wouldn't be knocked over. You will probably self-hug in private, however, maybe you will do it in front of others. You can be a role model for children, so they will learn how to do something so self-caring as a self-hug.

From Numb to Alive in Sixty Seconds

After repetitive work, strain, or not moving much, you may get numb. Muscle fatigue and motor sensory amnesia are other terms for this. When your body is constricted it creates low energy flow. If you ignore the pain signals long enough your neural impulses get exhausted and simply shut down. Numbness is one of your body's forms of protection. It allows you to carry on under duress or threat until you can get to a place to rest and heal. So don't let yourself pretend that numbness means you are pain free! It simply means your muscles are exhausted.

Later, when feeling returns it can be painful and inflammation from chronically numb or exhausted muscles can keep you awake. Prevent this by doing simple stretches in six to ten seconds as needed. Drop your arms to your sides and do this:

Stand up with your legs touching the front edge of your chair, feet flat on the floor. Bring your chin toward your chest, make fists with both hands, take in a breath, and lift your shoulders back and slowly up to your ears. Hold this position tightly for 10 seconds. Now release your fists and shoulders. Repeat this three times. Don't wait until you are in pain or numb!

Everyone Can Play When It's a Universal Playground

One day, after a particularly long day at my computer, I decided to go out for a short run-walk. Passing by the empty playground near our community center, I decided to go for a swing. Taking hold of the green play bars, I stretched out my stiff arms and shoulders. With the energy flowing back into my arms, neck, and back, I went from play area to play area. Find your own ways to play. For example, before I go upstairs sometimes I stretch on the post by the stairway near my office. Just make sure in choosing your playground that whatever you lean on is safe and stable.

I have learned lately that it takes one to have fun—
but two or more to have *comedy*.
—Marilyn Idle

Have You Smoothed Your Feathers Lately?

Smooth your own feathers as if you had them on your body. This move calms and uplifts your chi or energy. Lift your hands a few inches above your head palms facing your body. Now gently move your hands down around your head and body, while breathing slowly and deeply. Keep smoothing your feathers by wiping in a downward motion just barely touching your arms and legs. Give your calves, ankles, and feet a brush over. (Sit down if you need to, to do this.) Then finish by fluffing up your feathers from feet to head with ruffling motions: This will give an energizing lift to your now soothed and refreshed body.

Twist and Shout

One morning I woke up feeling stressed, mired in deep thoughts that seemed very important and serious. Then, a still small new thought came to me, namely, "Which of these thoughts would you like to play out for the rest of the day?" I checked the entire milieu of unhappy thoughts and found none I liked. My inner wisdom suggested, "Why don't you create some new ones in place of these? You can always return to the old thoughts again if you don't like the new ones." Just then, my husband said something to me and I reacted by blurting out some of these angry, serious thoughts. I felt bad to have spoken to him this way, and I let him know that I would find a new set of happier more helpful thoughts any minute. I had to go to town, so I said, "I'll feel better after I get back, and I'm sorry I shouted at you."

On my way to town the old Beatles song "Twist and Shout" came into my head. I sang it at the top of my lungs, and when I arrived home later that day the serious thoughts had been replaced with helpful caring ones—and then I shared them!

Whether you like rock, hip-hop, blues, salsa, belly dancing, ballroom or classical ballet, remember to turn up the tunes and find your *own* way to express your feelings on a frustrating day. If you're weighed down by troubling thoughts and feel like shouting them out, instead, use music to move into thoughts that *help* you! Music is one way to work out your pent up feelings before you express them, you might even scream or have tears. Turn up the tunes and find your *own* way.

I love this song, with John Lennon on the lead vocals. Remember, don't just read the words, sing (and loud)!

Twist and Shout (written by Phil Medley and Bert Russell)

Well, shake it up baby now
Twist and shout
Come on, come on, come
Come on baby now
Come on and work it on out
Well work it on out, honey
You know you look so good
You know you got me goin' now
Just like I know you would
Well, shake it up baby now
Twist and shout
Come on, come on, come
Come on baby now
Come on and work it on out
You know you twist, little girl
You know you twist so fine
Come on and twist a little closer now
And let me know that you're mine, woo
Ah, ah, ah, ah
Yeah, shake it up baby now
Twist and shout
Come on, come on, come
Come on baby now
Come on and work it on out
You know you twist, little girl
You know you twist so fine
Come on and twist a little closer now
And let me know that you're mine
Well shake it, shake it,
shake it, baby now
Well shake it, shake it, shake it, baby now
Well shake it, shake it, shake it, baby now
Ah, ah, ah, ah.

Giving and Receiving Thoughtful Support

This is a chapter about spending supportive time with the ones you care about.

It is easy to forget that the best things in life are free. Giving and receiving thoughtful support is one of the most enjoyable things you can do to make your day healthier and happier for you and the people around you. Do it every day with those you care about!

During turmoil many people tend to retreat, put up shields of self-protection, or turn away in pain, conflict, exhaustion, or exasperation. Yet, with a daily practice of giving and receiving thoughtful support through words, notes, or actions, you will make it easier to connect during unsteady times. When you have lots of daily experience in giving and receiving support, you will be ready, when you most need it, to face a challenge. Instead of clamming up and withdrawing you will be able to keep giving and receiving face to face, hand to hand, heart to heart, and hug to hug, with even deeper love, respect, and understanding for one another.

Bouncing ideas off each other generates new ideas.
Talking about something back and forth, in safety, openness, and honesty, no matter how hard it might be sometimes, can be very freeing. Besides finding solutions together, it can be deeply moving for each to know you are doing your best to help each other to feel cared for and loved—and to be fulfilled and happy!

Talk About It

When you and your child, partner or someone you care about have a troubling issue to deal with, even if you or they have been yelling or are now feeling hurt, get a glass of water or cuppa tea, sit down at the table, and look at the concerns. Eye to eye, heart to heart, powerfully, gently, and with mutual care, talk together. Take turns listening and talking and start over if you fumble. This seems easy enough, yet I know from personal experience in relationships that it isn't easy sometimes. We are all human and we don't always understand each other right away. If, while you are talking, you or someone else doesn't feel understood (and by understood, I don't mean agreed with) then ask again and clarify what each of you are trying to say. While you are talking together, avoid cutting each other off or taking the stage for too long!

Getting Support When You are Hurt.

Emotional pain can be invisible, but it is no less hurtful than a physical wound, and sometimes more so. People use up great amounts of energy covering unhealed hurts. Hurt feelings need to be given the same kind of attention you would give to a physical wound. How? By listening, being present, offering a cup of tea, a touch on the shoulder, a gentle back rub, or some comforting words.

A helpful person is someone who really cares about you, is willing to find a calm place and time to listen to you, can be trusted to keep your confidences, is understanding, and can empathize with your pain without trying to make it go away or fix it right away. A helpful person trusts that you will do what it takes to help yourself in your life or relationships step by step. She puts her own unhealed emotional upsets on a back burner for another time, so she can fully listen and be there for you. A helpful person is aware that emotions do actually heal, that pain goes away once acknowledged, and knows that the only place for you to go is back to love, calm, relaxation, and happiness.

It is important for you and others to understand limits and levels of energy. If there are too many deep pockets of pain bubbling up all at once, you may have to say, "For me to be here for you, I need you to find more support from other sources." You may need to set limits such as, "I have the energy to be here for you for one hour tonight, okay?"

Here is a note regarding what I call "great injury". Emotional, mental, or physical trauma can be locked in our memories and in our very cells. It may take more than a family member, friend, or partner to listen to these deep injuries. You may wish to find a mentor or counsellor who can safely and kindly listen and also help you release pain and decide what you need in terms of healing and healthy living.

Ask for What You Want!

It would be nice if your partner or family members were watching constantly to figure out how to give you care or a special gift. Often, they aren't. By asking directly for something that you would appreciate, those who love you can give you something that means a lot to you, and it makes them feel successful and happy too. Also, this helps them to know more about who you are and what you like. They see your self-caring role model and may learn that it is okay for them to honestly ask for what they would like to receive too!

Time Out! Don't Try to Solve Concerns When Tired or Tempers Are High

After many years of finding ideas to solve concerns in our family as they arise, pent up blowouts rarely happen. Yet, recently some feelings had built up about an issue we were struggling with and differed strongly about. Then it happened! The whole family had a raw, out in the open argument burst out, just before midnight when we all were exhausted, angry, and needed to get up early the next morning! One problem is that we were in separate rooms, shouting at each other, not calmly sitting at the table where eye-to-eye and heart-to-heart can help. Instead, we were throwing words at each other. Naturally, it took three times as long to express our concerns. Words were ricocheting in the air and intense emotions flew.

I stood in the hallway and yelled that we ought to stop and get some rest. "Let's start over tomorrow after a good night's sleep. There are still a few hours left to sleep." Finally, we did it! We stopped the unproductive arguing and went to bed though I'd had to scream it seven times like a traffic cop at an intersection, gently, powerfully reminding everyone that we would find a solution! All of us settled down and slept. Not surprisingly, an answer popped up by the time morning broke.

So, if an arrangement doesn't come quickly, don't continue arguing! If you have blurted out something nasty or immature, stop as soon as you realize what you did and say, "I'm sorry." Rationality can reach an all-time low when hurt emotions are high, if you or others are worn out, or when you lack enough information to continue. Don't waste hours going in circles. Before you ignore this good advice, remember, Einstein said the definition of insanity is "doing the same thing over and over and expecting different results." Instead of attacking, use your power to say, "It's all going to be good, because we will make it good. We will help each other until this is resolved. We are a family, in this together, and this family's story always ends in kindness, mutual love, and healthful solutions that everyone can live with. This problem won't go away by morning, so we can deal with it then!" (Unless of course it does dis-solve by morning!)

Being Right or Being Happy

There are two ways to argue. One is to find out who is right and that person wins while the other is seen as lower or wrong; the other is to find out what each person needs in order to feel respected and happy, and how to help each other get these things in a healthy manner.

Blanket Forgiveness

If little unacknowledged hurts have built up in your family, your partner, or a good friend, you may want to clear them up by offering a sincere deeply loving, "blanket sorry." You ask for forgiveness for all the hurts you have caused. I just say: "If in any way I have been insensitive or have hurt or insulted you please forgive me and let's start over!" This will not necessarily mean that all of the hurts are simply gone. You may still need to give some time and your mutual attention to clearing and healing the past.

I Am Sorry

If you hurt someone, say you are sorry. It's free. It's simple. It heals. Sorry is not so easy to say sometimes, but more often than not, say it anyway, especially to those you love, trust, and care about. Sincerely saying you are sorry is nourishing. It is like giving a hug.

When Your Sorry Is Rejected!

If someone rejects your apology, they may have lost a level of trust in you or the safety of the relationship. If the other person feels disrespected, not valued, or emotionally unsafe with you, *sorry* may not be enough. Stop and find out what it will take to rebuild trust.

You may wish to draw on clearing words like, "Help me to understand why you have lost trust in me" or "What will it take for each of us to show that we respect each other?" Share comforting and powerful words that support the two of you in this painful moment, like: "I love you and I love me. I value you. I value me. Let's do better next time to avoid hurting each other when we differ, okay?"

Forgive and Forget?

If someone makes a mistake I like to forgive quickly, but I do not forget what happened. Forgiving quickly frees me to have compassion, while I can still prevent a similar harm in the future.

When A Child Says, "I Am the Best in the World"

When a child says, "I am the best in the world" a knee-jerk parental response can be to say, "Don't brag." Maybe we're hoping to humble or correct our child, but it is better to say, "Yes, you are the only and best you in the world!" If you can say this to your child, you can also unapologetically proclaim to yourself that you are the only and best you in the world.

Don't Give Up

In an argument I don't give up and immediately accept another person's solution as being right or final. Nor do I stomp away offended, deflated, or angry (anymore) when a concern is unresolved. Sometimes you and the person you differ with may need to step away for a time and then come back, even several times. Stopping for a few minutes to regroup or to think about new input, allows you to rejoin each other with new ideas, input, and calm to powerfully and mutually resolve the concern.

> Do not be the one who gave up when you got close to what you wanted
> Be the one who not only got close but succeeded
> Then, be the one who went one step farther,
> Helping others with what you know—to succeed as well!
> —Marilyn Idle

Successful Relationships Are Works in Progress

I think we do the best we can in relationship, given what we know. However, even if what I know is right, it may only be right for me! If you wish to protect your relationship, ask, and learn to understand your partner, friend, or child—take the time to ask, and hear their thoughts or input to see what is right for them.

Asking for Support

Sometimes in relationship we are as close as two peas in a pod and we exchange care naturally. But when things get busy, there may not be as much time for mutual support. Don't wait until you are hurting to ask someone you love to share some care or support with you. You can offer a moment of mutual care or even ask for some specific comfort or support just for you.

I have found that being specific can help. If I am clear about what I desire, and how many minutes I want, even someone who is very tired or busy may say, "Sure, I can do that!" To my partner I might say, "Will you give me a three to ten minute backrub right now?" If I receive a no, I don't give up and walk away sad. (Okay, maybe at first, I do.) I simply begin to figure out how I will give myself care and say, "Thank you for listening to me and I love you." Then, I ask again but for later: "Would you be able to care for me with a three to ten minute backrub tomorrow at 7 PM? Nine times out of ten we happily find a time that works for both of us and I receive some wonderful care! My clear request shows them (if they didn't already know it) that they can ask me for comfort or support too.

Your Goals and Dreams Are Important

It is important to stand up for your dreams and goals. If you do not, who will? No matter what, champion yourself! Stand up honestly and powerfully when you are inspired. Healthy families and couples learn how to help each person reach their goals and dreams.

Cheer Someone Up Today

Although you may think it to yourself, taking the step of complimenting someone out loud or in a note or card can fall by the wayside when you are busy. I love to give and receive heartfelt appreciation. Most people do. Don't ever get so busy that you don't stop for five seconds to say, "I appreciate you in so many ways. Thank you." What could you say or do today to compliment or cheer someone?

Connecting

It's fun to get a nice note and it makes you feel good. Have you written a note to your partner or child lately? Write a note to them if you have not. While you are at it you could ask them to jot a note to you sometimes. A simple "Hello, how are you?" or "I love you" put onto a piece of paper is a welcome surprise. It is fun to get a written letter or a note even if only one line. If you like, put a little sketch or funny drawing on it.

Ask When You Need a New Idea to Help You

There was a time when I felt I had to figure out most things on my own, and *do* everything alone in working toward my personal and global goals and dreams. If this is the case for you, it is not only okay, but also important to ask others who have succeeded, or who have wonderful skills that are different from yours, for help!

Maybe you feel stuck, under-equipped, isolated, or you lack finances, emotional support, or confidence. There are many life coaches who have begun working during the past decade, and with the internet lots of free tips and advice are available. I have taken powerful steps in my life goals by saving up the money and hiring someone who is successful, even if just for an hour, to teach me something or give me advice. That hour can make a huge difference toward helping you get over a bump.

Everyone needs help at some point in life. I have learned over the years that many people who have reached their goals feel honored if you ask for their input. They will sometimes say they cannot help, but more often they will respond positively to your clear request for a moment of their time and a tip that really helps!

Family Meetings

I know from growing up in a family of ten that concerns, great ideas, or precious dreams can be left floating when things get busy or stressed. If this is the case in your family, even if all you have is two minutes to give, do it.

I wonder if this kind of thoughtfulness would lessen the billions spent on prescriptions for anti-depressants each year. I was shocked to learn that the drug companies are now testing anti-depressants for use on 7 year olds! A seven year old is just learning who they are and how to think and feel and care for themselves and to navigate and co-exist with others and nature on this beautiful yet sometimes muddled world.

Have a little talk that acknowledges a goal or concern as often as you can. Nothing may get done right away about the things you talked about in your two minutes, at least not right away, but maybe you, your partner, or child, will set a plan into motion as a result. Maybe these shared moments do provide enough time to co-solve a niggling concern, right then and there. Or, a bigger idea will grow from this meeting of minds and hearts, now in an honored and protected place. Will you take a few minutes today to talk with someone you care about?

We All Make Mistakes

All humans make mistakes. If you are hard on yourself when you make an error, whether little or big, *stop it*. Breathe. Most mistakes are inconvenient and maybe a bit embarrassing, yet if they are not life threatening, move on and do what is needed to start over. What's done is done. Whatever the *faux pas*, the first thing to do when you make a blunder, no matter how bad, is to forgive yourself—especially when your energy is low or you are emotionally exhausted (which is when most bad judgements, mix-ups, or mistakes occur). There is no point in pounding yourself. Instead, as quickly and calmly as you can, start over.

When mistakes or unhappy circumstances happen in your relationships, here is a checklist that may help:

1) Forgive myself.
2) Figure out what caused this mistake to happen.
3) Prevent further unhappy circumstances by saying, "Let's start over and I'll do better next time."

4) If needed, create new co-protections and co-understandings to prevent something similar from happening again (this helps rebuild trust).

5) As soon as possible, acknowledge the concern directly to those who are hurt and sincerely apologize.

6) Remember you are human, that humans make mistakes.

7) Know that where there is *love* there are second, third, fourth, and more chances to start over.

This is a note about life-threatening mistakes, lifestyle choices, or accidents preventing wellness or your success. If you are unconsciously causing yourself accidents or *too many* mistakes, most especially any that risk your life, relationships, or success, stop, look, and listen to that part of you! You might want to get the help of a counselor or mentor to add to your awareness and self-care skills, to look at what's going on, and to make self-protective changes in your behavior.

Don't Hold a Grudge

After a difficulty, stop and take a moment right away, or later that night, to talk about and fully resolve the upset. That way, you can both put it behind you and carry no grudges. Instead, you can hold each other in a compassionate hug, in understanding, peace, and happiness together!

Are Your Words Like a Butterfly Landing or a Hornet Sting?

If you want a butterfly to draw close or even land on you, what do you do? Communication requires similar presence and care. You can decide how you want your words to fly and land. To land well and be understood by someone you love, your words must always include some gentleness, especially if you and your partner are already experiencing frustration while sharing emotionally charged differences. Mutually protecting, respecting, and valuing, using powerful or gentle words and approaches, are always much more welcome than those that zero in to sting.

If You Feel Disrespected or Put Down

Most of us have been with someone who was so angry or hurt that they shut down, dismissed you, or began hurling insults toward you. Any two people can experience sparks flying in the beginning of a difficult conversation and this is healthy passion. However, some people protect themselves emotionally by taking pot shots at you or your values. What can you do?

First, you can watch insults like they were leaves blowing around in a windstorm. If they are not helping either of you, let them land but not on you. When insults start to fly, say this: "Let's calm down first so we don't hurt each other anymore. Then we can find a way that works for both of us." This type of statement can steer you both back to compassionate thinking, which can help you focus on and resolve the difficulties.

Talk During Change

Sometimes big or even little changes in your circumstances, finances, career, or health may rock you or your relationship more than you expect. Even amazing or positive change can bring stress. Do not let your anxiety or uncertainty cause you to withdraw or attack. You are in this together. Make a pot of coffee or tea, sit down, and talk as often as either person needs to. Share your thoughts, feelings, desires, and concerns. Most of all share mutual understanding, love, and support. This will help you face the changes together. Step by step, each person will feel happier, calmer and supported.

Use Protective, Not Attacking Words When You Are Angry

While you are upset, do not use words that attack the other person or your precious relationship. You have worked to build your connection, so mutually attack the problem, not the person who loves you.

Sometimes Relationships Change or End

Changing, evolving, growing, and yes, even separating and dying are all a part of life. It is okay for relationships to change or graduate to different levels and even as difficult as it can be, it is okay for them to end if life circumstances or choices cause your paths to change!

Major life changes can be large enough to seriously shift or end a relationship and that can be very hard. Have compassion for yourself and the person you love if you are experiencing this type of pressure. You can always love each other forever in your hearts. If lifestyles or uses of energy or time are too different to remain in relationship with someone, don't be hard on yourself or them. It is okay to say goodbye lovingly and honorably while respecting and valuing both people.

Remember too, that a goodbye can lead to a new kind of hello with new people, or a hello again with those from whom you parted in the past. You and they, people whom you love and who have grown separately for a time, can choose to meet again in a better way, time, or place!

When You Feel the Pain of Others

What the heaven! Why am I feeling this? More and more, I meet people who are becoming more sensitive to what is going on all around them, beyond their own lives and on the globe. If this is true for you, you may be able to feel others' hurts and even global sadness. Like birds, bees, dolphins and whales, humans feel vibrations. If you have checked into yourself and found the pain just doesn't seem connected to your life and present circumstances then it may be about someone else's heart aching.

You don't need to take a painkiller, tranquilizer, or drink to block out your sensitivity, as tempting as that may be! You can acknowledge the suffering you are picking up and send an "I am sorry" or "I love you" through your thoughts. Sometimes I imagine a compassionate comforter of love gently snuggling the world. It is big enough for all to curl up in. While I'm thinking about the ways I can make the world a better place, I sometimes reach for a warm comforter to wrap myself up in. Having my heart beating with love alongside of other hearts beating with love makes a difference.

The Butterfly and The Rubber Hammer

This chapter is a little story about co-respect and co-care.

There once was a boy who was only just four when he became so angry with his mother that for the first time she heard him say, "I hate you." Delicate tears welled up in his mother's eyes then rolled down her cheeks. With her body slightly quivering she replied, "It is okay for you to express your thoughts and feelings. I love you even when you feel angry and will protect you and me and not allow you to hurt me or you."

She kneeled in front of him looking up into his eyes and said, "There are more caring ways to express what you feel and you don't have to like these caring ways, yet, you must use them. You and I are different, sometimes as much as day and night. We desire different things and need to be separate from each other. You don't even have to like being with me. Even when we are apart we are still together creating our different goals and dreams. You are not allowed to hate me and I will not hate you. Some day you will understand why."

He picked up his toy rubber hammer and furiously pounded the ground. He looked at her with pain and anger etched on his face and he stomped away. A few moments later, he returned to her side saying, "Mommy, I feel hurt and angry." As she gently wiped his tears, she took a breath.

Then, as if nothing happened he declared, "Mommy, I missed you and I love you. Can I have a hug?" Quietly, she pointed to the tears on her face saying, "I feel sad right now. Soon my tears will stop and I will be able to give you a hug."

Looking into his mother's eyes, he took a step back. She whispered, "Part of me is delicate like a butterfly's wings. You cannot swing at a butterfly's wings with a hammer and expect it to quickly return and land on your shoulder. I need some time before I can open my soft wings." Then, with a giggle, she added, "I mean open my arms and hug you."

Watching her ardently, he listened as she continued in a soft voice that was music to his ears. "When you said you hate me tears began to fall from my eyes." The small boy dropped his toy hammer and walked over to her. Raising his hand and softly touching her cheek as he wiped one of her tears, he said, "Mommy, I am sorry I hurt your wings and made your face wet."

With that, she opened her arms and together they enjoyed a beautiful hug as she softly told him, "I always invite you to talk with me gently or strongly about how you feel and what matters to you. I will tell you how I feel and what matters to me. Neither of us will allow our words to hit, hurt, or harm. Whenever we express hateful words, let's stop and start over right away. We can start over as many times as necessary to understand one another with love and respect. If we use very powerful words, like a hammer, then the words must only hit the ground in front of each of us. Then we can both see and hear one another. That will lead to our co-loving and co-understanding each other."

"Co-co, co-co, co-co. I like co-co," he sang. "Can we have a cup of co-co after our hugging mommy?" She laughed and happily sang back to him, "Yes, yes, yes! I would love to have a cup of cocoa with you!"

—Marilyn Idle

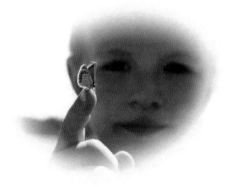

Coupleship

This is a chapter about finding your ways in your unique relationship to build meaning and the love and adventures you both desire in life-lasting relationship.

I didn't like my job. Not because I didn't love both people in every divorcing couple I met. The part I didn't like was I knew they still loved each other, yet were parting.

I was a mediator, a neutral person who helped

couples tally, take apart and divide the finances and belongings of their marriage, as well as helped them to mutually create co-parenting guidelines for the children. If the pain of sitting together in mediation was too great for a couple, they were then positioned for a fight they didn't deserve or need with lawyers in the court system.

In mediation, deeply personal things are revealed with the hope of fairly settling and sharing assets affordably, without lawyers or court. This helps honorably and co-respectfully end a marriage with as much understanding as possible. There were some who would misuse mediation. In their grief and hurt they would use information shared to bully their partner and then went to court anyway if the partner didn't yield to them. I did my best to discern who wanted to get on with a new life that was fair to both people and I worked with them. I kept them out of that courtroom!

I would say with honesty in every meeting, "You can't pay me enough money to help you fight against each other, so let's work together and use the least of your time and money as possible, so you two can get done what you both need to do with no further hurts or loss." I helped people honor their precious marriage, the time they had together and begin their new lives.

You may think this is a strange way to start a coupleship chapter. Yet, having a background in law, mediation and counseling, and now in wellness, I have seen too many people who still love each other, who have lost their path together, end up in court. My intent of this chapter is to share some of my insights and ideas about using self-care to care for your relationship so that *you* can stay together and graduate to each new loving, lasting, level of your unique union.

When Two Unique People Bring Their Worlds Together

What Is a Co-Couple?

Couples who share:
co-input
co-support
co-creating
co-understanding
co-sharing
co-love
co-trust
co-kindness
co-curiousness
co-solving problems together
and co-honoring of each other.

Being a co-couple means you are committed to caring for the two of you in all of your life's adventures in a way that loves, supports, honors and protects both of you. Recognizing that each of you may have very different preferences, needs, desires, dreams and goals and bring many non-financially definable energies, skills or gifts to your relationship and lives is equally important. Knowing this can help you to do what it takes to understand and to take turns in supporting each other over the years.

When conflicts come (as they do for everyone) you will have built mutual honor and a supportive bridge back to each other. If you are new to the ways of co-coupleship, then exchanging (and valuing) mutual co-input is one very important key to having successful adventures and a loving home.

No matter what you may face personally or together, ask each other daily questions like, "How are you?" or "What do you think?" and listen with care to the answers. Each person's viewpoint and who they are as a person changes daily and evolves with this kind of healthy exchange.

Co-input helps you see what is accurate about each other and your life circumstances each new day. As you graduate again and again to a new level of who you are personally and also as a couple together, tenderly ask to understand and be patient with each of your different ways of seeing the world. Sometimes, even when you are both using the same language, you may sound very foreign to one another. Most of us are from very different upbringings, familial or cultural backgrounds, and have views and values that are different, not wrong.

In co-coupleship, you consider both people's views and values and most often come up with a third view which encompasses the best of both your worlds. If you get upset take the time to talk when you are both calm enough. If you don't have enough time to fairly listen in the moment, in co-coupleship you arrange to find a time to listen to everything that matters to the two of you.

Some day you will be co-elders (and sometimes even co-colleagues in work and giving back to the earth on the various projects or stages of life), and in a co-coupleship you will have celebrated the best of life and co-living, supported every step of the way by one another. Each of you have grown in your different gifts, alongside one another, so, you can help the world be a better place, just by being who you are and sharing co-peace and co-laughter.

Count How Many Times You Read "Co" in This Tip

Then multiply that by the days you hope to stay in a co-coupleship. This is the kind of effort it takes to co-build your lives together in a manner that will last. So how many co's did you count? (Remember to multiply your answer one thousand times more ...with co-humor.)

Expectations

No matter how brilliant and superhuman your partner seems at first, no one is perfect. Be careful about putting your partner on a pedestal, especially in the early stages of your relationship. There is no place to go from god-like status, but down. Make sure that the expectations you have for the person you love and yourself are humanly possible and something you can live up to. There are going to be differences in opinion and some disagreements—you are human! Also, do not expect that your partner knows how you feel or what you think about something just because when you first met they seemed to know intuitively how to please you. When you are both talking about something important to you, make sure that you both really do understand the same thing. The single greatest waste of energy is failing to ask for clear input. The second is thinking your partner's silence means they agree with you. The third is predicting and expecting failure. If you must have expectations, then have these. Expect to always help each other to understand, to succeed in life, to be happy, and to be and feel loved.

Don't get married unless ...

Even if you are very in love and will never divorce, I believe it is important to think about and sort out how you will commit to support both of you in your lives, roles, work, play, finances and goals and dreams over the years.

I have seen so much unnecessary suffering within people's marriages and so many ending in divorce. It's not very romantic to think in advance about how you will protect and always help both of you, most especially if you ever chose to part from one another—but it is very loving.

In our marriage, with values, background, culture, views, upbringing and priorities which were very different, we agreed to talk and listen to each other every step of the way and it has not always been easy! We have lovingly found our ways to balance coupleship, family, finances, roles and taking turns to support each other's work, goals and dreams.

My own standard of protection before considering marriage was 100 percent love and 50:50 in the finances of coupleship, marriage and divorce, no matter who did what paid or unpaid work. My husband and I agreed we would not even bother to get married at all if we could not begin by agreeing to protect each other, our love and our relationship and home building contributions by co-valuing each other right from the start.

If you and your partner have not talked about some levels of your relationship which may now be concerning the two of you, lovingly and with thoughtful understandings and care for each of you, find a time to do so now.

> The trick to being a good nurturing hugger,
> is not to be the first one to let go.
> —Marilyn Idle

Learn New Communication Skills

If you are married, you might be aware that the divorce rate is nearly six out of ten. That is not a bad thing, as there is nothing wrong with not wanting to live for the rest of your life with one person, especially if it feels unhealthy to do so. I feel deeply grateful that during a couple of rocky spots in our relationship, my partner (kicking and screaming "I'm not going to counseling") and I decided to care more for our coupleship than our self-image.

We agreed to go even though each of us knew ourselves to be "right" and it was painfully obvious something was very wrong with our partner! We both were sure: "*I'm* not the one who needs counseling." Having the kind ear of a calm counselor supporting both of us helped us get through some confusing, hurtful places together, with new insights. Now that we have been humbled and have matured it is an honor to do whatever it takes to live (most often) happy and fulfilled, while always willing to find new, greater ways to understand, be friends, solve problems in a respectful way, or show love to one another.

I learned from experts in university and college courses and read hundreds of relationship books in my career, before getting married. One year after I got married, I threw away everything I had learned. The expert ways, rules and advice were not working for our life situations or for us! With our differences, dissimilar family backgrounds, diverse goals and dreams, and ways of communicating, we were foreign to each other and had to find our own ways to relate that would actually work for *us*.

The only thing that did work for us was to say "I'm sorry" when we hurt each other, or in my case, ask for an apology when my partner didn't know I needed one, and then, to start over with new insight and care from what we had just learned.

How to Feel Mutually Respected and Create a Co-respecting Home

At first, and in each new chapter of your relationship over the years, you may not always agree about what "home" should be. You can each add what is important to you from your own worlds or past family traditions yet also co-create what really works now, in a mutually pleasing home—a soft place to fall. A co-created home protects, comforts, and holds love for both of you.

When you struggle about your home, don't fight, but listen to each other and love each other's input. If you differ strongly, don't give up because the other feels stronger or is persistent. Each person's ways are only "right" for them, so, when co-living, being right is never more fun than being happy together.

When creating your home, create a place of relaxation and peace where you can simply be together and have your quiet times after the days and nights of life's work and adventure. Here is where you can tenderly meet and unfold your unique coupleship dreams or goals, alongside one another.

No Place for Harm

There is *never* an appropriate time in your relationship for abuse, whether physical, emotional, verbal, or spiritual. If you tend to escalate toward harmful behavior, whether passive or aggressive, then *stop*! Seek new skills to manage your anger right away, or go to counseling together for both of you. If you are unable to learn safer ways, separate temporarily. Mutual safety must come first and then each of you can find better ways to prevent or respectfully manage and show frustration. Whether your style is to passively smolder or to blatantly blow like a puffer fish that fills up with water becoming up to ten times its normal size and looks like a balloon with prickly spines, you and partner have a much better chance of happily evolving when you learn to redirect your powerful energy to calming and communicating passionately, yet in love and respect!

Find Your Way ... Together

If you are committed to being a couple, make no assumptions and let go of being right. You are two different people and must learn about the way that works for both of you in your life and circumstances. Living the love in your hearts is not always easy. You must be willing to find the answers that help you to find your way, *together.* This is possibly the most important and simplest way to help you both build a mutually fulfilling coupleship that lasts.

Both my husband and I are usually wonderful, generous, kind, loving, wise, supportive, curious, thoughtful people and more, yet during arguments and hurts, when we differ, our gazes become wide-eyed with bewilderment as we each momentarily forget that about each other. Over the years, in each new stage or chapter of relationship, and especially during difficult learning curves, one of the most important questions we have both learned to ask each other (sometimes with gritted teeth, and now decades later, more gently), "What is it that you want or need?" After we have figured that out, we can begin to create it. When an argument runs without resolve, now, one of us will eventually, stop and ask, "What is it that you want or need (and when and how can you, or we, find doable ways to create that for you)?"

The "D" Word: We Shall Not Speak of This Again

Every couple has their problems, and sometimes, the two of you will have passionate and even horrible arguments. For the sake of your relationship and the love you have for each other, keep your passive or aggressive anger under control and express it in healthy ways. When people are angry, hurtful words fly that are usually not even meant. However, after spoken, it is hard to take them back; the hurt is done. Learning to put up an emotional umbrella and to safely express difficult emotions with one another can help more than putting your foot in your mouth or stomping on your partner's toes. If you don't learn to keep your anger in check and talk things out calmly, rage or helplessness become entrenched and the word "divorce" can be easily thrown around.

If you don't want a divorce, *never* bring up the D word in your arguments. If you need to go to another room to cool off, do that, but whatever you do, don't allow your coupleship to become a bargaining chip in an argument. What you more than likely need is sanctuary, outside help, or

new skills to help resolve arguments. As you take rest, learn more, listen, and understand each other, the pains will dissolve. A useful D word *to* use when you are hurt or angry is "Delete!" Then add something like: "Let's start over. I'm feeling deeply hurt, scared, and angry and need peace and love again in our lives. Will you help me, us, to get through this?"

Starting Over

When you and your partner have a bad start in a conversation that has offended or hurt either of you (or if you are in an unhelpful shouting match), *stop* and start over. If you need to calm down first, do so. Then come back and start the talk over. You can each take time to calm down and then start over as many times as is needed. If your partner or you are notorious for leaving the scene of an argument and not returning, agree to stay in each other's presence as you calm yourselves. Or, if the topic is very heated, you both may need to set a time to return to talk later or the next morning.

No matter how hard it is to finally reach a solution honorably and safely, calm yourselves and come back to each other with new understandings until you do so. Hard as it is to believe, you *can* eventually get through this, if you both want to!

Bumps Along the Way

Unless your partner is doing something that is against the law, harmful, or totally irresponsible, the way to spend your energy when you get upset (if you do dearly love your partner, despite their faults) is to put it into learning the skills you need and getting the support you deserve to help yourself and your partner evolve in your coupleship. You would put energy into starting a new life or starting a relationship so why not devote this energy and get help for the one you have now? Spend as much time and effort as you need to learn about co-relating and learn how to stay whole, healthy, and empowered personally, while also continuing to co-build more ways to be together in love. There has been no coupleship book written for your specific circumstances. Others' supportive ideas, counseling, or books can help, yet the two of you must stop making excuses. Start over in mutual respect and co-write the happy ending book, which can only be written with love, by the two of you!

Open Your Eyes and Follow Your Instincts

Do not overdo this, but once in a while step back and take an overview of how your coupleship is going. Look at what is and is not working in your relationship. Are there definite skills missing or recurring problem areas that need to be understood better and co-resolved? Think about it. If you invest in a business you pay attention to what is going on so you can make changes if needed. Yet so many of us start out romantically, thinking that if we say the word love enough things will magically work out. And when things are going in a wrong direction, many people will simply keep going, increasing the forcefulness of their arguments or becoming more silent or distant, resulting in loneliness for both, even while standing near each other.

As already mentioned, but worth repeating in many frustrating life situations, Albert Einstein's definition of insanity, "... doing the same thing over and over again, expecting different results." So, stop doing what does not work, learn new skills, and take time daily to help each other co-solve problems with do-able ideas, with no one to blame while you evolve together. Listen to your gut feelings, yes, but bring new ideas into the open sooner rather than later. If you believe that something is bothering your partner or is not right in your relationship, keep it between you and your partner and work things out as a couple. But, if you need help, then find a mentor or person who is completely devoted to seeing you work things out and become happy and successful with each other.

When You Get Tired of Working on Your Relationship

Anyone can entertain the thoughts: "Where is the perfect partner in the universe for me? Relationships are supposed to be fun, right?" Everyone, at some point, must learn how to work things out in a relationship, especially if there are children. Never stop having fun, because in between every adventure you enjoy, there will be a next time where you will need to work on your relationship again. It's easy to think that by being alone or moving on to another person, you will find greener pastures or an easier partner. And you may find a partner who has different skills or qualities, yet you will still need to work through challenges, stresses, and arguments from time to time, and sometimes unexpected big ones!

Couples usually don't mind working at their relationship as long as they have fun and a way to get back to closeness to each other. So have lots of fun and celebrations and don't let working at it be more important than the happiness and play days!

Co-Creating a Fresh New Kind of Relating

Take a look at the way you talk to each other to see if that is really how you want to keep relating, especially if it is escalating disappointments or making you both unhappy. If you are accidentally replaying old patterns of relating that keep you limited, free yourself and your partner. You don't have to act out something anymore just because you know it predictably *from past experience* with your partner! For that matter, you don't have to become a mindless actor, in anyone's tired script or monologue, most especially *not* if it has a tragic or broken-hearted ending. Instead, bring your ideas together and co-create a better way of talking and celebrating happy successes and refreshing new ways to care for each one of you starting right now.

Compliment Each Other a Lot!

It is very common for people to notice something nice about their partner and keep it happily inside or even talk about it to others. Yet they never, or rarely, voice these wonderful observations and admirations directly to the one they love! Perhaps they think, "They should know I love and appreciate them." Ironically, many find it easier to share negative things! But, without the love, this is destructive and can very quickly weaken or tear a good relationship apart. Wonderful, loving compliments help to reawaken your love for each other and shore you up for the times when you need to share your anger or hurts!

Take notice of the good things your partner does and let them know frequently the fine person you think they are. Tell them that you see and appreciate them and the special things they do. The compliments I am talking about are not flowery or poetic words, unless you feel inspired to say or write them. (I would love to have a poem spoken to me, honey!) I mean genuine compliments, based on something your partner does that you truly appreciate. If you have had an argument and want to share a compliment when shields may still be up, you may want to say, "Even though you and I are feeling hurt and angry right now, I have not forgotten the wonderful, caring people we are, the caring person that you are!"

Mend Misunderstandings

If you don't regularly find a way to mend hurts with someone you care about, then stormy feelings between you can make the air feel thick. If you are playing out what seems to be an unending painful story, where you are the good guy and they are the bad guy (or the other way around) you can be fairly sure that you haven't mended misunderstandings and have buried them or built a wall. When you and your partner are feeling hurt or angry, communication can be the first thing to stop when you need it most. Or, actually, sex or nurturing kisses or hugs may be the first thing to stop!

From personal experience, I know that some days I have a tough skin, and other days I am tender and deeply hurt by what others do or say in an argument. If you have clammed up or withdrawn it is self-protective and natural to do that. However, take every step it takes to mend things. This will require that both of you let down your guard *without* throwing caution to the wind.

Here's what you can do:

Start to talk things out. They won't go away by ignoring them, like a cold war, or by rehashing them with more raw force. Make an agreement that you will talk about anything and everything. Agree that you will name anything unhelpful and call it a "vent." Listen only to the helpful words that calm and soothe after the hurt, attacks, accusations, or judgments have stopped. Listening well does not mean you are agreeing with everything that is said. However, if you differ about something, get it out on the table as soon as you can over the coming days. Calmly discuss each differing issue with co-respectful care, powerfully, and with gentleness, face to face. Then work out a co-protective solution. For most of us, this is painstaking. Yet doing this, in the end, leaves you both feeling much better and growing to the next chapter of your coupleship, loving and honoring *both people*.

Communication Under Stress

When sparks fly, simply agree to and use mutual care words or guidelines to protect and respect both of you during a conflict. These words are simple and you can add your own to the ones below.

1) Find a mutually agreeable time to talk and use mutual respect to talk about concerns and find out all of the details from both people.

2) If either person has a hurtful slip of words, don't rub it in. Apologize, take a rest, calm down, and start over, or if either person gets stuck, mutually agree to ask "Tell me more?"

3) If ideas are needed mutually ask, "What do you need or want?" Be specific with solution details: "When and how can we do this in a mutually respectful way?"

4) If either of you get tired, don't say, "You are such a wimp." Say thank you for how far

you have gotten. End your talk and set a new time to get together and finish.

5) Share mutual compliments if it has been a tough go. Keep regrouping until you finally co-resolve any concern with a co-solution, which means one that you can both do, and live, and be happy with.

Note: You do not have to stay in a relationship if it is too difficult or is harming your health. Yet, if you want to stay together, before you decide to leave, think about this. Maybe you and your partner *do know* how to communicate and *how to solve problems*. Maybe you both know *how to start over* with forgiveness. Yet, maybe you both did not know *how many times* you would need to do these things, whenever needed, for the rest of your lives!

After an Argument

Here are some clear ways of talking during a fight that can dissolve hurts and help get to a point of finding solutions that will help both of you:

- "I love you, I love me, and I love both of us. I also know that you love me and I know that you love both of us."
- "I want to understand you and what you want as much as I desire that you understand me and what I want."
- "I feel as frustrated as you feel and I want both of us to feel understood."
- "I want, and I think you also want, to find a healthy way to protect us both and to protect our relationship. Let's keep taking turns to help each other until we both feel happy."
- "Let's sit and cuddle or be together quietly for a while and talk again when we are both calmer, okay?"

Say these co-protective and co-caring words over and over when you need to. They invite care for both of you in order to soothe feelings, to stop wrestling, and help you both to start over. Do this for the rest of your lives whenever needed and say these kinds of things as many times as it takes for these co-loving and co-protecting words to sink in, to care for, and to work for both of you.

Say You Are Sorry, Right Then and There

Have the courage to say you're sorry immediately—even if you have to say, "I'm sorry *somewhere* in me. I sure as heaven don't feel sorry yet, however, I know I love you and I know I am sorry that we are both hurting."

Help Each Other to Lighten Up

Often, when couples have gone through or are going through some painful spots in their relationship, things can feel constantly deep and serious. It could be that there is an extraordinary amount of stress, or you are both so worn out you are afraid to ignite another fight with whatever you say. No matter what, find a way to lighten up. Do not take every glance, remark, or movement as a serious problem. If your partner makes a mistake after you think you have something resolved, let it go, or if appropriate, laugh about it. If you make a mistake, poke healthy fun at yourself. More often than not, this will start reducing the tension.

Stop Fighting and Write It Down

If, during a discussion, you find yourself whirling in overwhelm, find a piece of paper and write down a list of everything that is frustrating you. Then, you can take a breath and clearly form an idea about what needs to be attended to and how to go about it in a more successful way for you and the person you are with.

A Clearing and Caring Way to Talk

Many couples I have met have a special storage bin within which they keep painful, hurtful, unhealed experiences and memories near to the surface, which taint their ability to be together afresh. Here's a powerful and wonderful way to empty that storage bin before the *delete* button can be used effectively!

Find a good time for both people. You do not need to resolve everything all at once, nor always together, in fact, many times, you cannot. If either or both of you are busy, be very specific and clear and choose only one outstanding concern to clear up, so you can finally let it go. Use words like, "I need some help from you to finally heal and let this go. Will you have a cup of coffee with me? I would like your input and help." Continue to find times and ways to meet until you are both feeling relieved, understood, trusting and happy again.

If you are busy people, be very specific about a time when you can both sit down or walk and talk together. Don't give up. This is one of the most powerful ways to support both of you. After you have both set up a time, you can congratulate yourselves because that commitment to help each other is ninety percent of the solution.

Remember that to get a clear answer you need to ask a clear question: for example, "I would like some relaxing time together with you soon. What day and time can we possibly do this?" Direct, clear questions can help both people. Using co-respectful, self-caring questions again and again will help both of you to relax, laugh and share more hugs together.

Find a Moment to Be Kind to Each Other

Kindness is often left behind in a busy life. Even good relationships can lack little moments of kindness. If your partner is working outside on a hot day, make a glass of iced tea and take it to him or her, giving a tender kiss. If the one you love has been working at the computer all day, walk up behind them and gently say, "Save your work, I'm coming near you for one minute," and then massage their shoulders and neck. You get the idea.

Kindness means looking at the other person's situation and seeing what you can do to make it easier. This is a way to show your love and respect for each other.

Do Something Wonderful

There are little things you can do to surprise your partner, especially if you have had a disagreement. Little loving notes found in an unexpected place can mean so much. Even the moist stoic person melts a little when they find a love note on their desk or in their pocket or case. Give a small gift "just because," such as one chocolate wrapped in foil. These do not have to be expensive ideas whatsoever. A simple loving touch, playing with your mate's hair, rubbing their hand, a soft kiss on the cheek, a gentle pat on the leg, or giving a soothing back rub can make a huge difference in how your partner responds to you.

When was the last time you walked up to the person you love and without saying a word, affectionately placed a kiss on their nose? Not in a sexual way, but an affectionate way. The next

time the two of you are in your living room, the car, at a restaurant, or in the grocery store, quietly reach over and take your partner's hand. Don't be surprised if they pull back and you get a strange look of incredulity or curiosity, if it has been a while. Yet don't misread this startled look. You are doing something heartfelt, wonderful, mutually respectful, and fun.

If you can, have an overnight getaway, just the two of you, to some place off the beaten track where you can enjoy something new. A charming cottage with a fireplace or a delightful bed and breakfast may be ideal. Explore the area ahead of time and choose a place you want to walk or a café that the two of you have wanted to go to. Bring a nice

112

bottle of wine or pick up some hot cappuccino to sip while relaxing in front of a fireplace! Make this a friendship-building time, or if you both desire, a romantic weekend where you can relight your love.

Friendship Cuddle Time

Sexuality is a very special, exciting and ever so important part of being human. There is a time and place to be sexy and a time and place to simply cuddle and nurture each other. Each coupleship is unique, therefore, help each other by learning each other's understandable clues about how and when you want to be together sexually or non-sexually.

One of the most important loving couple care skills you can develop is finding how and when to cuddle and nurture and when to be sexually intimate together. Healthy, mature and responsible adults help each other to clearly understand the difference and respect that these two different ways of sharing love each have a time and place. This understanding creates lasting trust and mutual respect and a bridge to both of these precious ways of loving one another.

When you first met each other, being friends and cuddling might have been the way you showed each other you cared each day, and then your way of loving one another may have become primarily sexually romantic for a time. It is possible, if you are like many couples, that after a while both kinds of sharing—sexual sharing and non-sexual cuddling—may have slowed or even stopped, especially if you have children. If this is the case, take some time just to be friends and to cuddle again. If your partner is sitting on the couch watching the TV or a movie, or reading in bed, quietly scoot close and open your own book. This can make both of you feel good, secure, reconnected, and loved. Put your ear on each other's hearts and listen to your heartbeats. Then, when you are both feeling cuddled, trusting, and respected, gently talk about when and how you want sexual intimacy and find a way and time that works for both of you. Help each other in each new, fresh and evolving chapter of your lives, to find the right time, place, and mutual happy ways to share both of these special ways to share loving.

Ignorant Hurtful Outsiders

No one knows you and your partner the way you know each other. Do not allow other people to interfere with your coupleship. If friends or family members think you are hurting or stressed, they may "mind read" the problem and try to take away your stress by getting in the middle of your conflicts.

Though well meaning, this type of rescuing is usually not helpful and becomes an interference that can prolong the time it takes to co-resolve a coupleship problem. Although getting another person's input or perspective is not a bad thing, make sure it is only when you ask for it. It is very important to keep integrity, honor, mutual trust, and respected intimacy in your coupleship.

Working at Home

I have learned how hard my working at home all day and sometimes into the wee hours of the night can be on my family. While sharing work or some work experiences at home or with your partner is absolutely natural, living your work at home 24/7 is not.

If you have to have a home office or you bring work projects home, set a specific amount of time that it will take you to complete each night and let your partner know when you'll be available, and when stopping time comes, stop! It is important to separate the two parts of your life and keep your work schedule limited to be fair to and give care to yourself and your partner. If you must do your work, projects, or job at home, set very clear boundaries and set rest breaks and days off to pay attention to your partner and family. You can't do that if you are running on empty. My beautiful partner and our child reminded me of this very clearly while I was writing the chapters of this book!

Adore the Person You Love

Even though we still disagree and have fights I adore my husband and he adores me. It wasn't always that way. Yet, now we see there is no conflict in loving and adoring one another, as well as having different opinions that need to be co-resolved. Beyond telling your partner you love them (or don't like them when you are angry!), tell them they are special, that you admire the best of who they are, and that you are deeply grateful for all the good they bring to you and into your relationship. You can love the person, faults and all, even if sometimes you don't always like what they choose to do. This is cherishing your partner and your commitment to helping each other to shine. It shows that you see and adore who they are despite of your differences, and that you do not take them for granted.

Help Each Other

So often, after all the work there is little time for play. Help each other! A day can be whittled away by errands and chores. If you find that the amount you do is lopsided, ask your partner to help. On the other hand if your partner does more than their fair share, and they look frustrated while you relax, simply say you want to help and ask which of the jobs you can take over so they can relax or do something they want to do too. This, to me, shows a great depth of care. Sometimes if the time is right and weather is perfect forget the chores and go play. Not surprisingly, the household tasks will wait for you!

Spend moments together

Whether you have a whole day to share, a week or just five minutes, spend time together. Simply stop and be together, sharing sweet nothings or a kindhearted word or moment of your gentle silent love for one other.

Foods That Help Rebuild a Youthful and Fit Body

This is a chapter about eating scrumptious foods that protect earth and you! Included are mouth-watering organic recipes.

What foods can help you maintain youthfulness while you age with strength, wisdom, and grace? In this chapter you will find some fresh ideas about foods and drinks that keep you and the Earth balanced and vital.

Writing this chapter, I looked back many times to memories of myself as a small girl playing and learning about life on my grandparent's farm. When I grew up and went to university I moved to a polluted city where I lived for many years. By my seventh year there I had fifty allergies (which are all now gone). I became painfully aware of the insidious harm turning away from body-respecting food, living without fresh air, and taking quick-fix pharmaceuticals for every little ache could cause.

I once knew intuitively from what I saw as a child that the environment and our bodies are related and must be in harmony, yet having lost that innate understanding, I returned to self-empowered wellness and nature only just in the nick of time. I see ever more clearly that during those body-crushing years I was disconnected from the natural world and ignoring my inner loving self.

I learned the hard way that if you restore, build, and heal more often than you damage your body, you have a fair chance at keeping yourself alive and well for your lifetime! If you are like me and enjoy treats, coffee, chocolate, whipped cream, wine, and french fries, I invite you to balance those with foods that create health, especially if you have children.

And now, here are some helpful food tips and scrumptious recipes. Use people-ecology-animal friendly and fair trade ingredients whenever you can. Bon Appetit!

Fast Organic Multi-Layered Freshly Sliced Apples and Cheese or Tomatoes and Cheese

Very thinly slice your favorite varieties and colors of organic apples or tomatoes. Thinly slice your favorite cheese. Stack in layers.

Delicious!

Overfed and Undernourished

Eating is one of our most powerful and primal desires as well as our main source of nourishment. Until we get adequate nutrients, the hunger signal remains active. Eating a lot of non-nourishing food means we have many empty calories to store as fat. Our bellies are full yet we are nutritionally starving, even as we gain weight.

One solution is to build your body by whole plant-based foods each time you eat deadened chemically preserved fare! This kind of balancing self-care gives you freedom and fun with food, combined with the power to prevent life threatening diseases and premature aging with genuine nourishment.

Earth Stewards

I have a deep respect and humility for my grandparents, which I can barely find words to express. As a little girl they taught me about the role of bees, insects, and animals on the farm where everything lived in ecological harmony and was lovingly and humanely cared for. They were what we might today call organic farmers, and worked hard to bring beautiful nourishing foods to many people. Stewards of the Earth, they worked with soil, plants and farm animals, while respecting and living in balance with wild animals and nature.

There are new young farm families moving back to the land and learning organic or chemical-free farming in order to raise their children while caring for nature. Working long and hard hours similar to my grandparents, they provide sustainable food in their communities and are asking only for a fair income. In my view, one of the best ways to protect your family's wellness is to eat colorful foods that nourish you (and taste great!) from your own backyard, or from nature-respecting sustainable or organic farms in your region—food that has no need for a colorful box!

If you enjoy exotic foods from around the world, make sure they are grown in nature respecting ways and that they are fair trade. True fair trade protects the health of the farmers and their families and pays them a fair wage. Support these people who are using time-honored ways of working with Earth's ecology, who treat animals humanely, protect the soils, waterways, and you and your precious children.

Children and Local Sustainable Gardens

I listened to an interview on www.mercola.com recently, between Dr. Joseph Mercola and Dr. Shiv Chopra about Dr. Chopra's book *Corrupt to the Core: Memoirs of a Health Canada Whistleblower* where he talks about making our food supply safer with his "Five Pillars of Food

Safety." As Dr. Chopra explained, five of the most offending substances in the food supply are antibiotics, hormones, GMO's, pesticides, and slaughterhouse waste. He suggested: "If we demand that these five substances be removed from the food system, automatically all food becomes natural. We don't have to fight for it as organic; we don't have to label. We don't have to do anything."

They talked about how to break out of the corrupt for-profit, controlling and manipulating system that is destroying the food supply and said this would be done by putting the power to grow food directly into the hands of *children* and those caring for children, gardens, and small farms!

The idea of teaching our kids to grow food locally is bubbling up all over. My friend and organic farmer Kurtis of Wild Thing Organics in Christina Lake, British Columbia wants our schools to bridge with community to teach eco-friendly gardening. Dr. Shiv Chopra is involved in such a project in India where sixty percent of the population are small farmers, many now seriously harmed by severe corporate manipulation.

Would your children enjoy a community eco-garden as part of their learning at school? A place outside in the fresh air or in greenhouses where they can be self-empowered, connected with nature, and not just becoming enamoured with credit card debt, more things, or *consuming*? In a garden, they can grow while they grow their own food! They can tend it, harvest it, and even learn to preserve it through drying or canning! An experience like this would last a lifetime in their hearts and minds.

From the time I was a wee girl until I was seventeen years old, I learned how to plant seeds in my grandparents' greenhouse and then transplant the small plants into a garden field. While I could barely reach the clutch I steered an old red Farmall tractor through rows of tomatoes while my grandparents loaded filled baskets onto their flatboard wagon. Bringing gardening into our schools will powerfully teach and protect children as they discover the joys of touching nature through learning to feed themselves for a lifetime!

Get-Up-and-Go Energy Balls

2 cups peanut butter (or any nut butter)
½ cup liquid raw honey (or more to hold it all together)
1 cup chips (dark, milk, or white chocolate)
1 cup raw sunflower seeds
2 cups dried fruits (mixture of raisins, dried cranberries, or dried apricots)
1 cup sesame seeds (hulled)
1 cup old fashioned rolled oats
½ cup cocoa
½ cup of rice crispy or bran bud cereal to add crunch (optional)
1 ½ cups ground raw nuts or shredded coconut (for coating)

Use a wooden spoon or your hands to combine all the ingredients except the coconut in a large bowl. Roll ¼ cup scoops of the mixture into balls and then roll them in the coconut. Store in an airtight container in your refrigerator for up to a week or for two months in the freezer.

Perk-You-Up Coffee Bran Muffins

These not too sweet, melt in your mouth, touch of coffee muffins are great!

Makes 18 jumbo muffins.

You can store this batter in your fridge up to a week and bake a few muffins fresh each morning.

2 cups raisins
2 cups cold dark roast or decaf coffee (substitute milk and 2 more teaspoons of vanilla for the coffee if making these for children!)
2 cups cold pressed oil
5 (farm fresh or free range) eggs
2 cups milk (or milk alternative)
2 teaspoons pure vanilla
4 cups natural bran
4 cups all-purpose flour
2 cups sugar
2 teaspoons sea salt
2 teaspoons baking soda
2 teaspoons non-alum baking powder

Preheat oven to 350°F.

Soak the raisins in hot water to plump them up and set aside.

In a very large bowl combine the coffee, oil, eggs, milk and vanilla, and mix well. Add raisins to liquid mixture and stir.

In another large bowl combine bran, flour, sugar, salt, baking soda and baking powder. Add the dry ingredients to the liquid mixture and stir thoroughly. Using muffin papers or greased muffin tins fill 3/4 full. Bake in oven for 20 to 25 minutes.

Organic Rice Crispy Date Balls (Easy No-Bake)

½ cup butter (or cold pressed coconut oil)

1 cup sugar
1 egg
1 ½ cups chopped dates
1 tablespoon vanilla extract
7 cups crispy rice cereal

Place all except rice cereal in a pot or bowl and stir until thick. Pour liquid mixture over cereal and combine using your hands or a spoon. Roll balls in coconut, cocoa or nuts to cover and place on waxed paper or press into a buttered pan and top with a snowing of coconut.

Fruitsicle Smoothie

Freeze leftover organic peaches, strawberries, blueberries, or your favorite fruits. Blend fruit cubes, some ice cubes, organic milk, yogurt, rice, soy, hemp or almond milk, pure vanilla, and organic sugar or honey to make a creamy fruitsicle smoothie.

Baking Soda Tummy Soother

Drink a glass of water with a quarter to one teaspoon of baking soda mixed in it to help neutralize an acid tummy when you've overindulged in coffee, fatty foods, or rich sugary sweets.

Have Some Sunshine in a Tropical Food or Drink

It is important to eat sustainably and locally as much as you can, yet with the growing number of ecology-respecting and fair trade food growers around the globe, it is fun sometimes to enjoy exotic tropical foods from distant lands.

What drink would you like to enjoy while it fills you with the essence of the sunshine from the land on which it grew—some lime, orange, kiwi, grapefruit, mango, star fruit, papaya, coconut or pineapple?

Ultra-Healthy, Hearty-Invigorating, Super-Spicy Vegetable Bean Soup

Here's a very simple put-it-all-in-the-pot-and-simmer, immune-system boosting soup that will keep you warm during the cold months.

You will need:
Large cooking pot
A big spoon
Can opener
Something to store leftover soup in the refrigerator for a week or in the freezer for a month.

1 cup cooked red beans (or 1 small can)
1 cup cooked black beans
½ cup pitted chopped black olives
4 Portobello mushrooms chopped
4 cups fresh, diced tomatoes (or one 28-ounce can diced tomatoes)
1 4-ounce can tomato paste
2 cups diced fresh carrots
2 cups chopped fresh broccoli
2 cups chopped fresh spinach

These are herbs and spices you can use dry or fresh, and in whatever amounts please your taste (or choose your own favorites): Basil; cilantro; cayenne pepper, garlic, green chile pepper, jalapeno pepper, oregano, rosemary. Top with shredded cheddar cheese, raw sunflower seeds or cashews, and serve with a fresh slice of bread (or toasted garlic bread). For extra heat, serve with a splash of hot sauce.

Put all ingredients into the pot, set the heat to medium, cover and stir occasionally until it's piping hot. This makes about ten large servings so you may want to store some in the freezer for a busy day. Like all soups, this is even more flavorful the next day! This soup is loaded with protein, minerals, vitamins, fiber, and antioxidants. It is anti-mold, antifungal, antibacterial, antiparasitic and anti-heavy metal (chelating).

Sugar

How much sugar do *you* eat?

Even many "healthy" foods are loaded with sugar. Sugar consumption is up by almost two thousand percent in the last hundred years! How does this affect our bodies, emotions, and minds as they struggle to keep the blood sugar balanced in the face of this onslaught? Let me count the ways!

Your body's organs and systems are constantly working to rebalance your blood sugar. This includes pulling calcium from your bones to reduce the distress of over-consuming this acidic wonder called sugar. Once you learn more about it, I hope you will choose nature's candy more often such as fruits or natural sugar substitutes such as honey or the sweet leafy stevia plant, which has thirty to forty-five times the sweetness of sugar. The leaves can be eaten fresh, or put in teas and foods. Nancy Appleton, PhD, author of the book *Lick the Sugar Habit*, lists hundreds of modern health problems related to overuse of sugar. Prolonged over-use of sugar will disturb your alkaline/acid balance, your hormones, and your body's ability to produce insulin. It impairs your immune cells and attracts overgrowth of your body's "janitors," bacteria and yeast.

Some people love salty foods; I love sugary ones. And if you are like me, even after reading about how sugar can harm you, you still want to continue to enjoy sweets! So do enjoy them, but also, be balanced. There is no need to overdo sugar in a way that causes serious damage to your body. Simply reduce the amount of sugar you eat each day, eat *lots* of raw vegetables and proteins, and drink alkalizing lemon water before or after eating a treat.

Natural Non-Chemical Sweet Alternatives

Did you know the average North American eats 100 to 175 pounds of sugar in a year? Could this possibly be you or someone you love?

If you are going to eat highly sweet foods or drinks, consider using natural alternatives and NOT artificial "sugar." Natural sweeteners allow you to enjoy sweet taste without the harmful effects. Stevia and Agave are two sweeteners that are gaining a lot of appreciation. Stevia is a flower, a sweet herb which is a chemical-free sugar alternative with zero calories. It can be useful for those with low blood sugar because it stabilizes blood sugar in the body, lowers blood pressure and protects teeth and gums. Agave syrup contains the same amount of calories as sugar, but is natural unrefined fructose from the Agave plant. It is considered safe for diabetics to consume, lowers cholesterol, and is great for cooking. However, "safe" has been reported by some researchers to be at 25 grams or less a day. Use in moderation and to reduce a high blood sugar alarm, eat protein, such as seeds, nuts, beans or hemp seeds, before or after having your sweet.

Common sense and self-care balance would say eat less sugar, say, fifty pounds a year or less, depending on your current wellness, weight and activity level. This helps you prevent or reduce sugar or acid-related cell-deteriorative and inflammatory dis-ease states like arthritis. Eating less sugar eases insulin reactivity in your body and reduces high and low blood sugar swings. Also, you avoid storing fat, which is precisely what insulin does—it turns excess blood sugars into stored fat if your body does not need the energy.

If you want to eat sugary treats once in a while (and who doesn't!), choose the best quality sweets, chocolates, desserts or drinks and savor them, between balancing your body with pure water and nourishing foods.

Bypassing Bypasses and Avoiding Plagues!

My grandparents both lived into their nineties, simply yet abundantly on a small farm, always giving back to the Earth. My grandfather, who was very close to nature, never saw a medical doctor until the last days of his life. My grandmother, a powerful woman of the Earth, drove their orange pick-up truck into the city to market twice each week. Yet near the end of her life she became a passive receiver of drugs and surgeries and then her suffering began.

I believe imbalances were created from these approaches to aging. For their whole lives Grandma and Grandpa had been robust, and in between their arguments, tired from hard work, they were calm and peaceful. I believe they had wellness and longevity because they stayed close to nature, fresh air, clean water, herbs, vegetables, fruits, and the land.

Fast Organic Fresh Fruit in Pastry

2 cups all-purpose flour
1 ½ teaspoons salt
¾ cup cold unsalted butter, cut into bits
6 or 7 tablespoons ice water
Fresh fruit, nuts, sugar and spices

In a large bowl, whisk together flour and salt. With a pastry blender or your fingertips lightly blend in butter until mixture is course. Add ice water, one tablespoon at a time, tossing with a fork to incorporate, until mixture begins to form dough. On a floured work surface knead dough in three or four forward motions with heel of hand. Form dough into a ball and flatten. Put dough in covered bowl and chill one hour. Pastry dough may be made one week ahead and chilled. If you don't want the cleanup of rolling out the dough, just press the dough into square or round muffin pans. Or, buy some pre-made Greek-style pastry called filo, which is a very thin strudel layering-type of pastry and very easy and fun to use. Add sliced fruit, nuts, sugar and spices. Bake thirty to forty minutes at 350° F until fruit is tender and crust golden.

The Wellness Food Bridge

Food freedom and informed choice is important and if you are like more and more people, especially if you have children, you are on the new bridge to food that is nourishing and eco-sustainable. Many people are adapting tasty family recipes now using delicious foods grown in balance with nature. The deadened foods that once seemed fun to eat and affordable to buy aren't. If you look at a whole picture—dye-injected, terminator or gene modified, taste manipulated, whatever-a-coated and irradiated foods can end up costing you a lot more than your family budget! You can prevent the costly diseases associated with eating bad foods, have the freedom to be well, and have more money left over to have fun.

Carefully choose how you spend your hard-earned dollars on food for you and your children. Buy from food providers who profit in your wellness and happiness and who are body and earth respecting. If you want a lifetime on earth with those you love, being happy in a well body, then buy foods and drinks that are grown in sustainable ways.

Big Loser or Big Spender?

If you carry extra fuel (fat on your body), don't decide to lose weight, decide to be a big spender of excess fuel! Say to yourself, "I will be eating today in a way that doesn't store more body fat, instead, I am spending the body fuel I already have."

No one really likes to be a loser. Most of us, however, do like to use resources or be a big spender once in a while. When you or someone you care about is trying to lose weight, try this. Shift your intention and change your words. This simple change of phrase, a loser of body fat to a spender of body fuel can shift what seems like the burden of losing something to the excitement and pleasure of spending your fuel!

Many people say, over and over, "I am *trying* to lose weight." Remember, no one really likes to lose anything, so switching (deleting) your intent and words to say something like, "My body knows how to be the perfect size for me," or, "I am spending this extra body fuel that I have on my body." Here are some more spending words: "I am having fun eating a little less, while I have adventures and use up this fuel." Your brilliant body *will* know what to do and how to use the fuel. While spending your stored body fuel, eat many small meals of protein, fruits, vegetables, and sips of lemon water all day long.

Scrumptious Chocolate Strawberries

Melt your favorite fair trade chocolate. Dip strawberries into it!

One in Three

One in three children in North America are obese. A fourteen year old friend of our family saw me writing this tip and said, "Even if you eat too much one day, how hard is it to get off your tush, go for a walk and burn it off?"

Here are some good food and living tips for kids that will help to un-do obesity and create well-balanced and happy bodies and lives!

- Eat dinner together as a family (at least) several times a week.
- Eat crunchy, colorful vegetables and fruits and drink a glass of water before you eat value-less dead "fun" foods!
- Have an 80:20 rule: eighty percent good food and activity and twenty percent for such things as junk food and techno-playing-sitting.
- Get enough sleep. Sleep helps bodily systems work well. Your exciting life and world will be still there to enjoy next morning!
- Make sure you are calming, chilling out, getting ready for sleep, without lights, beeps, games or TV, at least an hour before bed.
- Cut down on graphic violent games, horror movies or valueless television. Limit your own negative TV or movie watching or game playing to twenty percent of your time or less!
- If something is nagging at you, talk about it. Talk with people you care about and see what you value or don't value as a person and family!
- Ask yourself what kind of person you want to be. What kind of food and body care do you want to have? What do you want to do or not do next?
- If upset lingers, over-stressing you, this can lead to empty feelings and then overeating to fill up! Instead, fill up with love and fun and self-care.

- Don't let silly terrifying movies, violence or scary images linger, causing you to get out of balance. These things can bring on emotional eating. Calm yourself. Talk and delete what you don't need. Find pleasurable, adventurous, fun, self-caring ways to figure out and get what you need!

Tropical Fruit-Juice Popsicles

Freeze some organic fruit juices of your choice in paper cups or ice cube trays with wooden stir sticks or small spoons in them to make natural, yummy treats. Do not add diet chemical sweeteners or chemically altered no calorie sugar (especially for children). Variation: On hot days, if you like a cool, luscious dessert, dip some peach, mango, banana or strawberry slices into melted chocolate. Place in freezer and serve when firm.

Organic Deliciously Simple Asian Noodle Salad

4 cups cooked noodles (hot or chilled)
Firm Tofu (optional) (thinly sliced)
½ red pepper (julienne)
4 leaves romaine lettuce (shredded)
1 cup carrot (julienne)
½ cup cherry tomatoes

1 small zucchini ((julienne)
½ red onion (thinly sliced)
parsley or green onion (chopped)

Dressing:
1 teaspoon chili sauce (or chili peppers)
1 teaspoon lemon juice
1 teaspoon rice vinegar
1 tablespoon olive oil
1 tablespoon Tamari soy sauce
2-3 tablespoons honey
2 teaspoons plain yogurt (optional)
2 tablespoons raisins (optional)
½ teaspoon salt

Mix all dressing ingredients and pour over noodles and vegetables, garnish and serve.

Chop-Chop Zen Rice Salad

Assemble the following ingredients, wash, chop and mix together:

1 cup red pepper
1 cup cucumber
1 bunch green onions
4 cups purple cabbage
1 cup carrots
1 cup peanuts
2 cups cooked brown rice

In a separate bowl, mix together:

2 tablespoons sesame oil
6 tablespoons peanut butter
6 tablespoons Tamari soy sauce
6 tablespoons rice vinegar
2 tablespoons finely minced fresh garlic
2 tablespoons finely minced fresh ginger

Pour over the chopped vegetables and rice mixture and chill for an hour or so before eating to allow the flavors to meld. Delicious and so healthy!

Avoid Sugar on Hot Days to Keep Cool

On the hottest days, sugar can make you hotter. Often, one energy drink, electrolyte drink, sweet soda drink or iced cappuccino has ten to thirty teaspoons of sugar in it! Though they are cold, ice cream, slushies, and milkshakes can have a heating and acidifying effect. Even though your tongue may for a moment feel cold, your blood sugar rises and your systems are heated and inflamed. You don't have to give up icy sugary treats. Make iced tea or coffee with just the perfect amount of sugar to meet your tastes. Try this:

Fast Organic Coffee-Lovers Cappuccino or Coffee Smoothie

Put leftover organic coffee into the freezer in ice cube trays. If you are not making a coffee smoothie that day, put the coffee cubes into a storage container or double bag in the freezer to keep them fresh. When you want a dark rich coffee smoothie, mix the cubes with milk and some organic sugar and blend until very smooth. Enjoy!

Fast Frozen Ripe-Fruit Organic Ice Cream

Chop and freeze until firm your favorite very ripe fruit. Place in blender with organic milk or milk alternative like coconut, hemp, rice or soy. Blend to desired smoothness. To be fancy, serve in wine glasses garnished with organic whipped cream or soft tofu whipped into a fluffy cream with vanilla. Top with an orange slice and mint leaves. Enjoy with a cup of sweet mint tea.

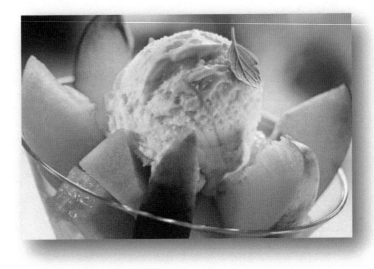

Get Back to the Future:
Become a Backyard Farmer!

There is a place again for the small or patio pot gardener and backyard farmer! If you do not already, you can learn to grow some of your own food. Some of the best sustainable food-growing ideas come from those who plant and harvest in ecology-stewarded soil and water, close to home. While you garden and eat, do it with gratitude and humility. Give your kindest care, respect and reverence to any form of life you grow and eat to recreate your own body. Protecting the diverse seeds and animal ecologies in your own back yard is how you and I, and seven billion other people, can go back to the future.

Fast Fried Wild Blueberry Pie

Place organic butter or a touch of cold pressed oil in a frying pan and fry as many small tortilla

rounds on both sides as you have guests. Keep warm in the oven on low. Using the same frying pan on medium heat, add more butter, some organic brown or white sugar, and blueberries. Sauté the blueberries just a touch, until warm but still firm.

Place the oven warm tortilla rounds on dessert plates. Heap on some hot blueberries, then splash with a little brandy or Grand Marnier. Top with a drizzle of organic cream and a touch of cinnamon.

Delightful!

Green Tea Shortbread Cookies

It's sweet teatime with these simple elegant tea cookies. These cookies are crisp and delicate and the recipe below will make a mildly sweet cookie. Increase the sugar by one to two tablespoons if you are a sweet tea lover.

2 cups organic all purpose flour
½ teaspoon sea salt
½ cup organic sugar or powdered sugar
3 teaspoons organic finely ground green tea leaves (or you can use black pekoe)
1 cup salted organic butter, softened
½ teaspoon pure almond extract
Fine sugar, for sprinkling (optional)

Combine dry ingredients in a small bowl. In a large bowl, beat the softened butter with an electric mixer just until smooth. Add the pure almond extract, then all of the dry ingredients. Divide the dough in half and shape into two circles. Put in a covered bowl. Chill the dough for an hour or two in the refrigerator, or until completely firm.

Roll the dough to your desired thickness (for small cookies, about one-eighth inch) on a floured board. Lightly flour the top of the dough before rolling. Cut with cookie cutters into your desired shape and arrange them on parchment paper-lined baking sheets. They expand very little, so there is no need to leave much space between cookies. Sprinkle a thin coat of fine sugar over the cookies (optional).

Variation: Substitute lavender buds for tea. To make a lemony-lime version of this cookie add the finely grated peel from one half of a lemon and one half of a lime. Bake in a preheated 325° F oven, for ten to fifteen minutes, or until lightly golden.

Fast Tortilla Organic Pizza

Preheat the oven to 350° F. Place pita bread or tortilla rounds onto a baking sheet. Drizzle with cold pressed organic olive oil. Grate your favorite cheese and sprinkle on the rounds. Thinly slice onions, garlic, green or other colored peppers, mushrooms, and tomatoes and lay them in that order evenly on top of the cheese. Chop and spread fresh oregano and basil over the top and finish off with freshly cracked black pepper. If you like spicy pizza, sprinkle with cayenne flakes or add a small amount of sliced hot fresh or pickled peppers. Bake for fifteen to twenty minutes or until vegetables are tender and the cheese

is lightly browned. Enjoy with a glass of organic red wine.

Organic Luscious Lemon-Lime Giant Muffins

In a large mixing bowl, combine the following organic ingredients until blended:

1 ½ cups sugar (adjust up or down to your own taste)
1 cup butter
3 eggs
3 tablespoons poppy seeds (optional)
1 tablespoon lime juice
1 tablespoon lemon juice
1 ½ teaspoons almond extract ("sweet" almond allows less use of sugar)
1 ½ teaspoons vanilla extract
1 ½ cups milk (or milk alternative)

In a separate medium bowl, combine the following three ingredients:

3 cups all-purpose flour
1 ½ teaspoons non-alum baking powder
½ - 1 teaspoon salt

Add the flour mixture to the liquid mixture just until moistened. Pour into lined large muffin pan. Makes: six large muffins. Bake at 350° F for twenty-five to thirty minutes, or until a toothpick comes out clean.

In a small bowl, combine glaze

1 cup icing sugar
1 tablespoon lime juice
1 tablespoon lemon juice
1 teaspoon vanilla extract
½ teaspoon almond extract
Zest of lime and lemon (shredded colorful part of the peel)

Drizzle glaze over warm muffins. Cool ten minutes before removing from pans to wire racks.

Variation: Replace citrus and poppy seeds with your choice, such as fresh fruit or berries.

Food for Thought: A Carrot or Cow Is Not Only a Product; It's a Life

We must all ask one of the hardest questions of all: "How can I (after my well lived life), give back, with gratitude and honesty, my precious body (my infinite love, once in form), back to the earth's cycles and systems of creation? How can I give my body, my seventy percent water and thirty percent minerals, healthily back to the soils and waters of the earth?" This may be a hard thing to think about, yet to do so is responsible and spiritually mature. You and I do eventually return to the earth and our bodies do become water and minerals again for other life.

No form of life, in the end, is higher or lower than another. Our body, when we have shed it, will form minerals and soil and water and give life to the grass, which feeds the cows that will happily and without shame munch on the grass grown now by your minerals and water after you have returned to infinite love. No different than when I once drank the cow's milk in its temporary earthly being-ness for a moment in time. I will express loving for *all* we are, were, will be, in infinity, in humble respect.

Crispy, Melt-in-your-mouth Organic Chocolate Cookies

1 ¼ cups butter (Yummy alternative: use cold-pressed coconut oil)
1 cup brown sugar
½ cup white sugar (or less to taste)
½ cup cocoa
2 eggs well beaten
1 tablespoon vanilla extract
2 cups flour
½ teaspoon salt
1 teaspoon baking soda
2 cups chocolate chips
¾ cup chopped nuts (optional)

Variation: Add ½ cup of broken up dark chocolate thin mints.

Cream butter and sugars, add eggs and vanilla and beat well. Stir flour, salt and baking soda. Add to first mixture and mix well. Add chocolate chips and nuts last. Spoon out by rounded tablespoonfuls onto greased cookie sheets.

Bake at 350° F for ten to fifteen minutes or until golden brown. Remove to wire rack.

Makes about two-dozen large cookies.

Homemade Italian Pasta Sauce

I have heard that a professional Italian chef worth her salt, will never use canned tomato sauce when she has the time and ingredients to make a fresh homemade one!

In a hot skillet, put 2 tablespoons organic extra virgin olive oil. Sauté 1 diced onion plus 3 garlic cloves, crushed with a large knife, then thinly sliced. Add 1 cup diced, fresh basil, ½ cup red wine, and if you have 6 large good field ripened tomatoes, blanch, remove skins, dice and add. (Or you can use 1 - 28 oz. can crushed or diced tomatoes.) Add 1 tablespoon raw sugar, 1 teaspoon lemon juice (optional), 3 tablespoons brandy (optional) and season with salt and freshly ground black pepper.

For me what really makes homemade sauce awesome is that you can add heaps of intensely flavored ingredients like capers, sliced ripe olives and herbs like Italian parsley, oregano, rosemary and cayenne pepper flakes. Add your favorites and simmer for a least a half hour. Serve on top of your favorite pasta along with a slice of fresh Italian bread and a glass of red wine!

Yum!

Italian Eggplant Caponata or Paté

Peel and dice 1 large eggplant. Toss with salt, put in a colander and let sit and drain for at least a half hour.

In heated skillet, sauté eggplant in 2 tablespoons of organic, extra virgin, olive oil with 1 small chopped onion, 3 cloves garlic, flattened with a large knife, then thinly sliced and a stick of celery, also chopped. Add 1 cup homemade Italian pasta sauce (or 3 ripe, diced, field tomatoes), ¼ cup sliced, black olives, ¼ cup chopped, fresh basil, 3 tablespoons capers. Season with salt, freshly ground black pepper, ½ teaspoon cocoa powder, pinch of raw sugar and add ¼ cup red wine or 3 tablespoons wine vinegar. Simmer for ten minutes, then cool. Garnish with fresh oregano or a pinch of cayenne pepper flakes (optional). Pulse in a blender for a few seconds, if you prefer a smoother paté. Serve on bite-sized pieces of fresh Italian bread. Antipasti deliziosi!

Enjoy!

Say Thank You to the Unseen Others Who Grow and Bring You Food

Before eating a sumptuous meal or drinking your drink, you could choose to say thank you in your own heart and mind. You are thinking about the people who played a role in growing, harvesting and finally getting the food to your food market so you could take it home. Send thanks to the unseen others. Say, "Thank you very much to everyone who had anything to do with getting this precious and beautiful food and drink to me!" or "I thank all involved, whether a precious person, animal, vegetable, nature, or the elements, that allowed this food to come to me. Thank you for caring about me.

Raw Avocado Soup

If you like soups such as Gazpacho you will love this very tasty, refreshing and delicious, raw avocado soup. It is incredibly healthy and highly alkalizing. Cut 2 tomatoes into small pieces and put aside. Put into blender, the flesh of 2 avocados, 2 celery stalks cut into pieces, 2 cups of fresh spinach and 2 teaspoons freshly squeezed lemon juice, sea salt or Himalayan salt to taste, freshly ground pepper and water for your desired thickness. Mix well on high. Pour the soup into a soup bowl and then add the tomato pieces. This serves two.

Enjoy!

Balance Your Body with Foods

It is intelligent and self-caring to consume both alkaline and acid foods daily to be well and balanced. To successfully neutralize (buffer) acid in your body, you need a store of alkaline material. Consuming seventy-five percent alkaline ash-forming foods and twenty-five percent acid-forming foods will help you to build a reserve.

Your blood pH is about 7.4. When pH levels in your bodily fluids vary too far out of optimal range, your body urgently goes through a variety of corrections to try to right the acid or alkaline imbalance. Blood that is too acidic gets sluggish and sticky and cannot efficiently transport oxygen to all of your cells. Chronic acidic states can come about when you eat, overall, too much acidic food, such as cola, sugar, coffee, denatured foods, meats, dairy and too little alkaline foods, such as fresh greens, vegetables and fruits. Over the long run these imbalanced states can damage you, your cells and organs and interfere with bodily and cellular reproducing functions. Your body's entire living processes depend on an alkaline inner ocean, and over-acidity is like pouring a cola into your goldfish bowl daily. Poor fishy!

If you do not keep your body at the right pH daily "acidosis" can interrupt cell activities and bodily functions—from the beating of your heart to the communications in your brain and nerves. Over-acidification depletes calcium and minerals from your bones, starves cells of oxygen, causes premature cell death, overloading of your lymph system, and overgrowth of bacterial and fungal "clean-up" activity that causes wonky cell growth and tumors. Eating a good deal of garden fresh foods neutralizes acidosis and therefore safeguards your cells' healthy functions and protects the minerals in your bones. Acidosis may explain why rich countries that consume the most calcium supplements and milk products, while also eating the most acidic foods, and eating the least fresh alkaline vegetable foods and drinks, also have the highest degenerative diseases, cancerous activity, bone breakage and replacements, along with escalating organ transplant rates!

What can you do? Be thoughtful, and balance acidic foods with alkaline vegetables, fruits and drinks; balance rest and activity; do self-massage daily to keep your body cleansing systems functioning and flowing; occasionally drink one-half to one teaspoon of baking soda in a glass of water to de-acidify an acid tummy quickly. As a child, when I had a candy-filled acidic tummy, my Grandma Pearl made me a little glass of this alkaline drink, and later in my life, I remembered that wisdom and am glad I did! My grandma lived into her nineties.

Here is an Alkaline-Acid Food Chart which will help you choose enough alkalizing foods daily to keep your body balanced, youthful and well!

Alkaline-Acid Food Chart

ALKALIZING FOODS	ACIDIFYING FOODS
ALKALIZING VEGETABLES	**ACIDIFYING VEGETABLES**
Alfalfa	Corn
Barley Grass	Lentils
Beets and Beet Greens	Olives
Broccoli	Winter Squash
Cabbage	
Carrot	**ACIDIFYING FRUITS**
Cauliflower	Blueberries
Celery	Canned or Glazed Fruits
Chard Greens	Cranberries
Chlorella	Currants
Collard Greens	Plums**
Cucumber	Prunes**
Dandelions	
Dulce	**ACIDIFYING GRAINS, GRAIN PRODUCTS**
Edible Flowers	Amaranth
Eggplant	Barley
Fermented Veggies	Bran, wheat
Garlic	Bran, oat
Green Beans	Corn
Green Peas	Cornstarch
Kale	Hemp Seed Flour
Kohlrabi	Kamut
Lettuce	Oats (rolled)
Mushrooms	Oatmeal
Mustard Greens	Quinoa
Nightshade Veggies	Rice (all)
Onions	Rice Cakes
Parsnips (high glycemic)	Rye
Peas	Spelt
Peppers	Wheat
Pumpkin	Wheat Germ
Radishes	Noodles
Rutabaga	Macaroni
Sea Veggies	Spaghetti
Spinach, green	Bread
Spirulina	Crackers, soda
Sprouts	Flour, white
Sweet Potatoes	Flour, wheat
Tomatoes	
Watercress	**ACIDIFYING BEANS & LEGUMES**
Wheat Grass	Black Beans
Wild Greens	Chick Peas
	Green Peas

ALKALIZING ORIENTAL VEGETABLES
Maitake
Daikon
Dandelion Root
Shitake
Kombu
Reishi
Nori
Umeboshi
Wakame

ALKALIZING FRUITS
Apple
Apricot
Avocado
Banana (high glycemic)
Berries
Blackberries
Cantaloupe
Cherries, sour
Coconut, fresh
Currants
Dates, dried
Figs, dried
Grapes
Grapefruit*
Honeydew Melon
Lemon*
Lime*
Muskmelons
Nectarine*
Orange*
Peach
Pear
Pineapple
Raisins
Raspberries
Rhubarb
Strawberries
Tangerine*
Tomato
Tropical Fruits
Umeboshi Plums
Watermelon

*Although it might seem that citrus fruits
would have an acidifying effect on the body,
the citric acid they contain actually has an
alkalinizing effect in the system.

ALKALIZING PROTEIN
Almonds
Chestnuts

Kidney Beans
Lentils
Pinto Beans
Red Beans
Soy Beans
Soy Milk
White Beans
Rice Milk
Almond Milk

ACIDIFYING DAIRY
Butter
Cheese
Cheese, Processed
Ice Cream
Ice Milk

ACIDIFYING NUTS & BUTTERS
Cashews
Legumes
Peanuts
Peanut Butter
Pecans
Tahini
Walnuts

ACIDIFYING ANIMAL PROTEIN
Bacon
Beef
Carp
Clams
Cod
Corned Beef
Fish
Haddock
Lamb
Lobster
Mussels
Organ Meats
Oyster
Pike
Pork
Rabbit
Salmon
Sardines
Sausage
Scallops
Shrimp Scallops Shellfish
Tuna
Turkey
Veal
Venison

Hemp Protein
Millet
Tempeh (fermented)
Tofu (fermented)

ALKALIZING SWEETENERS
Stevia

ALKALIZING SPICES & SEASONINGS
Cinnamon
Curry
Ginger
Mustard
Chili Pepper
Sea Salt
Miso
Tamari
All Herbs

ALKALIZING OTHER
Apple Cider Vinegar
Bee Pollen
Lecithin Granules
Molasses, blackstrap
Probiotic Cultures
Soured Dairy Products
Green Juices
Veggie Juices
Fresh Fruit Juice
Mineral Water
Alkaline Antioxidant Water

ALKALIZING MINERALS
Cesium: pH 14
Potassium: pH 14
Sodium: pH 14 (salt)
Calcium: pH 12
Magnesium: pH 9
Sodium Bicarbonate pH8.2 (Baking Soda)

EXTREMELY ALKALINE
Lemons
Watermelon

ALKALINE FORMING
Asparagus
Cantaloupe
Cayenne
Celery
Date
Figs
Fruit Juices
Grapes

ACIDIFYING FATS & OILS
Avacado Oil
Butter
Canola Oil
Corn Oil
Hemp Seed Oil
Flax Oil
Lard
Olive Oil
Safflower Oil
Sesame Oil
Sunflower Oil

ACIDIFYING SWEETENERS
Carob
Sugar
Corn Syrup

ACIDIFYING ALCOHOL
Beer
Spirits
Hard Liquor
Wine

ACIDIFYING OTHER FOODS
Cocoa
Coffee
Ketchup
Mustard
Pepper
Soft Drinks
Vinegar

ACIDIFYING DRUGS & CHEMICALS
Aspirin
Chemicals
Drugs, Medicinal
Drugs, Psychedelic
Pesticides and Herbicides
Tobacco

ACIDIFYING JUNK FOOD
Coca-Cola: pH 2
Beer: pH 2.5
Coffee: pH 4

** These foods leave an alkaline ash but have an acidifying effect on the body.

EXTREMELY ACIDIC
Artificial Sweeteners
Beef
Beer

Kelp
Kiwifruit
Limes
Mango
Melons
Papaya
Parsley
Seaweeds
Seedless
Watercress
Passionfruit
Pears
Pineapple
Raisins
Umeboshi Plums
Vegetable Juices

Breads
Brown Sugar
Carbonated Soft Drinks
Cereals (refined)
Chocolate
Cigarettes and Tobacco
Coffee
Cream of Wheat (unrefined)
Custard (with white sugar)
Deer
Drugs
Fish
Flour (white wheat)
Fruit Juices with Sugar,
Jams,
Jellies,
Lamb,
Liquor
Maple Syrup (processed)
Molasses (sulphured)
Pasta (white)
Pastries and Cakes from White Flour
Pickles (commercial)
Pork
Poultry
Seafood
Sugar (white)
Table Salt (refined and iodized)
Tea (black)
White Bread
White Vinegar (processed)
Whole Wheat Foods
Wine
Yogurt (sweetened)

UNKNOWN FOODS
The following foods are sometimes attributed to the Acidic and sometimes to the Alkaline side of the chart.
Asparagus
Brazil Nuts
Brussel Sprout
Buckwheat
Chicken
Corn
Cottage Cheese
Eggs
Flax Seeds
Green and Herbal Tea
Honey
Kombucha
Lima Beans

Maple Syrup
Milk
Nuts
Organic Milk (unpasteurized)
Potatoes, white
Pumpkin Seeds
Sauerkraut
Soy Products
Sprouted Seeds
Squashes
Sunflower Seeds
Yogurt

Chart Information Courtesy of:
Essense-of-Life, LLC. http://www.essense-of-life.com/moreinfo/foodcharts.htm

Organic Grandma Pearl's Salty Oatmeal Cookies

1 cup butter (or ½ cup butter, ½ cup cold pressed coconut or sunflower oil)
¼ cup brown sugar
1 cup white sugar (or less to taste)
1 egg well beaten
1 teaspoon vanilla extract
1 cup unbleached flour
½ - 1 teaspoon salt (to your taste)
½ teaspoon baking soda
1 teaspoon non-alum baking powder
1 tablespoon cinnamon (optional)
2 ½ cups oats (use old fashioned rolled oats not instant)
1 cup raisins (optional)
Chopped pecans, walnuts or any nut you like (optional)

In a large bowl cream butter and sugars, add eggs and vanilla and beat well.

In another bowl stir flour, salt, baking soda, non-alum baking powder and cinnamon.

Add to first mixture and mix well. Add raisins, nuts and oats last.

Spoon out by rounded tablespoonfuls onto greased cookie sheets. Bake at 350° F for ten to fifteen minutes or until golden brown and edges are crisp. Remove to wire rack. Makes about two-dozen large cookies.

How many ways can I send you love?
Let me not count the ways
Instead, I send you *all* the love there is *now*
And then, we can share it now and forever
Again and again
Every time, in every place we meet.
—Marilyn Idle

Unshakeable Peace

This chapter is about taking time for calm and peace.

You do have a choice.
—Marilyn Idle

Many people carry cell phones, Blackberries, iPods and the like and rush through work, chores, and responsibilities, trying to get it all completed, trying to do or to finish as much as they can each day, speeding along to get to appointments, rushing to do the shopping or get to events, driving as fast as they can in their vehicles to the next destination, rushing to do what needs to be done there, and then leaving so they can speed to their next destination. (Used to be me.)

Sadly, for many, they don't unplug or stop until they get sick, lose a relationship, or arrive at their *concluding destination* and understand what madness it has all been.

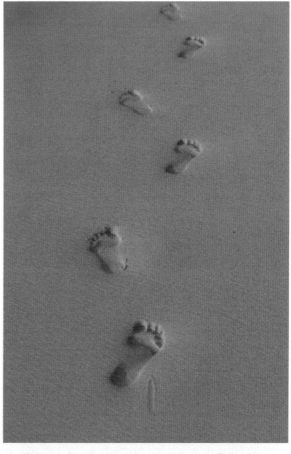

Life Doesn't Have to Be That Way

If, at the end of the day, you are often exhausted and stressed from the high-speed rushing and chaos and you don't have time for what's important to you, change it. You *can* find your way to live a simpler life. You and your partner or family *can* downsize and then take pleasure in doing only activities that you thoughtfully choose to keep in your life. Even while you must be busy some days, with a simplified life you will be present and mindful and take *peace breaks* in between.

Peace does not yell at you.
Peace does not put you down.
Peace does not rush you.
Peace does not feed hate to you or others.
Peace offers honorable self-empowered comfort.
Peace supports and protects you in your freedoms.
At your infinite center you *are* peace.
—Marilyn Idle

Have Unshakable Peace

Instead of thinking you can actually finish everything so you can *finally* have contentment, peace, and happiness, take some time now to really look at what is meaningful to you and your family. Contemplate what matters to you and talk together about how to make your life, your home, every step you take, every drive you take, every task you do, essential and connected to bringing you unshakable peace right *now*.

You may have gotten to this realization in your life, before you picked up this book. If so, you do know what to do (or more accurately, what not to do!*).* To have peace now, make time for peace—and every single day for the rest of your life!

I'll Have a Double Scoop of Delicious Nothing, Please

If you are like most people, your days may be overfilled with thought and activity. It's okay to stop and say, "No thanks. I'll have nothing right now. Yes, you heard me right. Absolutely nothing for me just now please." A moment of pure nothing is like having a scoop of the finest vanilla ice cream that simply melts and goes down smoothly and brings such sweet simple joy to a child. Have a double scoop of *delicious nothing* whenever you feel like having a moment or two of sweet re-treat.

Terra Means Earth

In many languages, terra is the name for soil or for the planet Earth. We can get terrified or *terra-fied* on Earth. One thing that makes this happen is not being aware of who and what we are beyond Earth's fields as part of infinity. If you can recognize yourself as a being that exists beyond Earth or terra as well as a person, then having a life and death as a human being can be less terra-fying and more terra-playing … and infinitely more fun. You are human, yet at the same time, you are a universal and peaceful part of Infinite Love. After I got curious about infinity, I have felt freer, safer, and more peaceful ever since. You can be the infinite, brilliant, beautiful and peaceful part of you even on terra—an awesome idea to ponder.

Peace, a Soft Place to Fall

Everyone on the planet deserves a peaceful place or home in which to be. Everyone deserves respect and safety and to be able to enjoy a center of peace. Take some time to look around at your home to make sure you have fashioned your soft place to fall, because your happiness, love, and peace ripples across the planet and this helps all others to find and build *their* soft place to fall.

Kindness Brings Peace

I do not think there is anyone who does not like to be treated kindly and as special. In relating to those you love or even to others you do not know, it takes no more time to be quietly kind, than it does to think negative thoughts or shout at someone, unkindly. If you realize in your tiredness or busyness that you have been unkind (as we can all do), press the delete button and start over in peaceable kindness.

This moment of nothing is for you.
—Marilyn Idle

138

How to Have a Peaceful Moment on a Planet Experiencing Such Turmoil

A peaceful moment is a moment of choice. This sunset at the lake photo was taken by my friend, after a fierce thunderstorm. We do have to "weather" storms and that is part of living on earth and I suspect almost anywhere you go in the universe. Yet, no matter what is going on all around you, in that moment, even during those storms, we can find within us a safe haven. Choose something peaceful and you become peace—even while on this sometimes wild and crazy ride on Earth. Fill up with peace and not only can you peacefully navigate your life experiences, you can also, just by your presence and by doing nothing, resonate peace and caring to others.

Love Loves to Love

I don't think there is anyone on the planet that doesn't seek love, want love, and deep down *know* love.

How can we perceive and be and know the infinity of love on a planet where people regularly fall *in* and *out* of love; where people often share love easily but then withdraw it just as quickly; where others may love us but then must leave us, or sadly, their life ends? I have found, for me, the way to know infinite love consistently is to understand that everything on this planet, secretly, is *made of Infinite Love.* Everything and everyone has always been and still is a part of Infinite Love in one state or form or another. Everything. No exceptions.

Your Inner Space

If you cannot get away from those who are noisy and frenzied, those who just don't understand why you need peacetime, even when you may tell them so, what can you do? You can surround yourself with your own rejuvenating peaceful thoughts and quiet peaceable energy. Breathe more slowly and deeply. When you are quiet and you slow your breathing down, you are in your own energy and can enjoy inner peace. This state can actually attract those who need just the same kind of peace yet may not yet know how to *be* it.

Peace and Quiet

In this technologically noisy world, several times a day, I find some way to have a moment of blissful quiet. Wouldn't it be nice to have a few moments of quiet in your day? No TV, no phones, no humming motors; just a moment or two of quiet. If you cannot get that kind of quiet in any corner of your home or office, consider finding a few moments alone in a spot that is the least filled with noise. Also, for a few small coins you could get a pair of earplugs!

If You Need to Step Out of a Noisy Place

No matter where you have to be, here are just a few ideas to get you thinking your way back to the center of peace. Say, "Please excuse me. I will be back in a moment." Go to a quiet place for a moment to get back to peaceful you. Put your hands under a water faucet imagining yourself standing near a clear river or waterfall. If you are at your desk imagine being in a rowboat, rowing across a glassy still lake. Find a private moment and place your palms over your eyes to rest them or give yourself a ten second embrace with a self-hug! Take a piece of paper and draw a circle and write your name in it and tuck it in your pocket, thus reminding yourself to take a peaceful moment as often as you need to. If you have not let others know why you need to be peaceful or quieter than usual, you may want to write them a little note saying, "Just resting peacefully for a few moments. I'll be back in ten minutes."

A Note for Children

If you have been crabby to others while trying to get a moment of much needed peace, especially if you have been short with a child who just cannot understand that you need space or quiet time to refill yourself, write them a little note or draw a picture of a happy face with eyes closed, resting. For older children, you could say something like, "I need time to fill myself up with love," or, "I need to recharge my batteries. They are low, a two out of ten, like a slow toy!" or, "I am calming myself down with peace for a few moments." If it is a new baby that you need to take a moment away from to calm or rejuvenate, you could ask a friend or family member or hire a babysitter for one hour to be there taking care of your baby while you are at home on the sofa or in your room.

Peace in Your Home or Workplace

What can you do to enhance your peace if you must spend long hours in a high-rise office building, noisy factory, or shopping mall? Don't lose your peaceful self, appeasing the

140

demands of agitated others or adjusting to a boisterous place. If you need a minute of peace, surround yourself, in your mind's eye, with an invisible *coat of peace*.

Tranquility in the Garden

I think of my flower garden as a place to provide me with peaceful comfort and quiet, a place to relax after a busy day or to pop out to visit during my day if I am working at home. A small easy to care for garden, for me, is also a remembrance-bridge and draws me back to nature and to my inner peaceful nature. Some people enjoy a rock garden. I have a small one with only stones and one large rock in the middle and a tiny metal frog sits on top of the center rock. I am always amazed at how peaceful a no-maintenance stone and rock garden is! If you don't have a garden, or even if you do, consider it not just a place to work in or to watch the flowers, or to grow and harvest food. When you need peace, you can you rise early just to be there, to enjoy your garden before heading off to work or after returning from work. You will find it a wonderful place to unwind. Your garden is a place of serenity that can help bring you to a state of peaceful calm.

Peaceful Ideas for Your Home

If you are like most people in this fast-paced world, you may find that it is easy to get stirred up by the outer world, and difficult to calm down and find your way back to peace. Building a tranquil spot in your home, or several little peace places around your home, can help you return to relaxation and peace. You can make your regular sitting places sanctuaries in your home by moving the TV out or moving your favorite chair far away from places of loud noise. Take some time and look around each room in your home to make sure you have places to be peaceful or to sit in which are in the best locations to promote calm.

It is easy to bring peaceful calm to you and your eyes within your home by making little charming areas where your eyes can softly fall as you walk about. You can place little mementos and treasures you find or have received from someone who loves you. Place small plants and this will add relaxing nature and greenness or flowering touches of color to your home. I have a colored rock I picked up from the beach that I place near me, on a windowsill, bookshelf, or table. It is so soothing to walk by these serene places. If I am in one spot for a while I love to light a candle in a glass jar.

Have You Had a Proper Stress Releasing Cup of Tea Lately?

Sometimes, even when I am alone, I like to bring out my biggest teapot and make a nice batch of brew. Please know that you can take time out for yourself at any time of the day or night to sit and relax with "a cuppa" tea or two.

Peaceful Ideas for Outside Your Home

Earlier in this book there were ideas to connect with nature by bringing in small stones and rocks into your home. Another thing you can consider doing is to bring one large rock into your yard or onto your patio or deck. Or you could gather varying sizes and build miniature sculptures by setting several rocks on top of one another. To bring a peaceful ambience to the outside of your home, stones can be used for footpaths or around a tree or plants. If you want to stroll into your garden at dusk or after dark you'll want to think about getting some solar lights for illumination. If you will be outside for a while you can light candles to provide a gentle flickering light. (Make sure you are always nearby and place them far away from tree branches or anything flammable.) Finally, put up some tinkling wind chimes in your backyard, patio, or garden to add a gentle, peaceful relaxing sound.

Do Nothing for a Whole Day

When was the last time you took a whole day to just be with yourself and do nothing? You deserve it. Join me and do nothing for a whole day. Find your day and just *be* with *you*.

Life is ever changing
Moment to moment
Season-to-season
Year-to-year
Find ... peace
Create your sanctuary
Make room for special times
Find wonderful places where you can relax
Have calm and peace and ...
Have scrumptious care,
For *you*
—Marilyn Idle

What a world this will be when we see that every man, woman, and child—and everything that is
on Earth—are infinite universal friends.
Oh, what an exhilarating world this will be.
—Marilyn Idle

Thank you to ...

Adele Neudorf, R.M.T., for your wise woman thoughtfulness, humor, care and friendship.

Catherine Hart, *Catherine Hart Communications,* author and bringer of uplifting joy, (who deciphered "Marilynese") and her husband John, in Taos NM, for their love and support. (... And for Chop Chop Zen Rice Salad!)

Danna and Brandon O'Donnell, *O'Donnell's Garden Market and Organic Farm* in Grand Forks, BC, for your care of the waterways, soils and airways and for growing such beautiful organic flowers and food.

Jan and Dan O'Flaherty, *Southern BC and Christina Lake Vacation Rentals,* for your care for me and my family and for so many families to whom you provide ecology-responsible vacations.

Karlee Bowman, photographer, for smiles, fun and for taking all photos of author and photos of Danna at O'Donnell's Organic Farm, Grand Forks, BC.

Kurtis and Karen Staven, *Wild Thing Organics Farm* in Christina Lake, BC, for your friendship, for co-respectful care of soils, rivers and forests and for your gentle stewardship of nature and animals in your raw milk cow share dairy.

Laureen McLean, photographer, for your friendship, love and care for nature and for photographs: footprints at Galapagos and summer sunset after storm, Christina Lake, BC.

Mike and Mickey Nadon, *From the Hearth Bakery* in Christina Lake, BC, for organic ingredient delectable pastries and hand-shaped breads, which I enjoyed eating while writing this book.

Nettie and Jeremy Lack of *Mad Dog Farms* in Thrums, BC for teaching me the word "whateveracide" and for sharing your joy of ecology-friendly, family, farming.

Nicole Pesta and Maya Pankalla from istockphoto.com, for fun, insightful help with photographs and input for the book cover design; and to the photographers at istockphoto.com and the precious nature, people and families in their photographs.

Pamela Leigh Richards, *FlyWithMeProductions.com* in Sedona AZ, filmatographer, photographer, writer, poet and *dancer on the beach* for your support and friendship in the infinity of love.

Stacey O'Donnell, dance teacher, in Christina Lake, BC, for reading and giving loving input.

Tom Cox, *www.Montalk.net, for* book design and publishing encouragement ... and for his music.

Paul Idle, my wonderful husband, for caring for, loving and supporting me, for reading, editing and giving valuable suggestions regarding care and protection of Earth's biosphere.

Nathan Idle, my great son, for editorial assistance, for love, hugs, support and humour.

... Marilyn Idle with her husband and their son, cat and Chihuahua lives in beautiful BC, Canada. You can visit her at her website: www.MarilynIdle.com.

Scrumptious Self Care Notes ...

31010930R00083

Made in the USA
Charleston, SC
03 July 2014